CHURCH

GATE OF HEAVEN

GORDON MOORE

Ark House Press
PO Box 1722, Port Orchard, WA 98366 USA
PO Box 1321, Mona Vale NSW 1660 Australia
PO Box 318 334, West Harbour, Auckland 0661 New Zealand
arkhousepress.com

Cataloguing in Publication Data:
Title: Church Gate Of Heaven
ISBN: 978-0-6454596-4-7 (pbk.)
Subjects: Leadership; Church;
Other Authors/Contributors: Moore, Gordon J

Published with Gordon J Moore
PO Box 46 Aspley Qld 4034 AUSTRALIA

*"And upon this rock I will build My church;
and the gates of hell shall not prevail against it."*
Matt 16:18

"IN GOD'S HOUSE"

Words and Music by Sonia and Steve Ryan

Deeply planted in God's House.
Where dreams flourish, where hope is found.
What I am giving will never fade,
What I am building will always remain.
This is where my heart is.
This is what I'll treasure.

I will always build Your House.
I will always find you here.
I will always cherish the love I've found.
Living in God's House.

Planted forever in this place.
Part of God's family.
Part of something great.
Home is where the heart is.
I've found my eternal home.
I will always build Your House.
I will always find you here.
I will always cherish the love I've found.
Living in God's House.

CONTENTS

DEDICATION

This book is dedicated to the church of the Lord Jesus Christ; the people who Jesus loves and gave Himself for, and, like everything that God creates, "*it is GOOD...it is VERY GOOD!*"

It is written to declare the Good News that our Lord Jesus Christ has provided a local church family for every child of God to be part of.

God's plan and provision of the church is that we would never be alone in this life. We are called, saved and set free to live a blessed life in Christ in our local church family!

"God sets the solitary (lonely) in families:
He brings out those who are
bound into prosperity:
But the rebellious dwell in a dry land."
Psalm 68:6

We were created by God to live in community where our faith can be practically lived out with others, together in the house of God, the church.

> *"Now therefore you are no longer*
> *strangers and foreigners,*
> *but fellow citizens with the saints,*
> *and of the household of God;*
> *And are built upon the foundation*
> *of the apostles and prophets,*
> *Jesus Christ himself being the*
> *chief corner stone."*
> *Ephesians 2:19-20*

WE'RE BETTER TOGETHER!

ACKNOWLEDGEMENTS

"If I have seen further than others,
it is by standing upon the shoulders of giants."
Isaac Newton

The contents of this book are part of the story of a 54 year journey which began in New Zealand after a personal, dramatic conversion to Christ in 1968.

A few years later in 1971, at the age of 18, I moved from my home town in Napier, Hawkes Bay, to the city of Palmerston North, to study education at the Palmerston North Teachers College and Massey University.

It was there that I became a member of the "Awapuni Christian Fellowship", which later became the "Palmerston North Christian Centre" church.

I realize many years later, that I had joined a church that

was experiencing revival. This humble suburban, local church would grow in size and influence from small beginnings to impact New Zealand and other nations. I am so thankful to God for the privilege of being part of this incredible story.

My new church family was led by a group of young leaders, called "elders", most in their 30s, who God miraculously brought together from many different backgrounds to lead this amazing church.

The key leaders in this group of elders (today we would call them the 'Executive Pastors') were Ken Wright, John Walton and Colin Campbell. Their love and passion for Christ and His church set such a wonderful example that has continued to influence me over the past 54 years.

I acknowledge these amazing leaders and pastors who pioneered, initiated and established new ways of doing church together.

Their beliefs, values, concepts and discoveries about the house of God became the foundations for our church in Bridgeman Downs, Brisbane, Australia, which we pioneered in 1986.

When my wife and I planted the church in Brisbane we

simply continued to do church as we always had back home in Palmerston North; Sunday worship and hospitality meals from house to house, praying and worshiping together, generosity in giving, supernatural Christianity, winning lost people, reaching this generation, making disciples and raising leaders, and above all, having fun together along the way!

This is New Testament church life in action.

"And they continued steadfastly in the apostles' doctrine and fellowship, and in breaking of bread, and in prayers. And fear came upon every soul: and many wonders and signs were done by the apostles. And all that believed were together, and had all things common; And sold their possessions and goods, and parted them to all men, as every man had need. And they, continuing daily with one accord in the temple, and breaking bread from house to house, did eat their food with gladness and singleness of heart,

Praising God, and having favor
with all the people.
And the Lord added to the church
daily such as should be saved."
Acts 2:42-47

This pioneering, apostolic spirit of constantly imagining new ways of doing church creates such a vitality, authenticity and momentum in church life that people are simply attracted and drawn into it.

Most of all, I acknowledge our heavenly Father and our Lord Jesus Christ, for creating the genius and wonder of the church, the House of God.

"And He has put all things under His feet,
*and gave Him to be the **head over***
***all things to the church**,*
Which is His body, the fulness
of Him that fills all in all."
Eph 1:22-23

Gordon Moore
AUTHOR

INTRODUCTION

The Church has always been preeminent in God's thinking and plans for mankind. God's House has been a central theme from the book of Genesis to the book of Revelation. However, to the casual observer this truth may not be obvious.

In 1982 I wrote my first book on the church, in a manual, teaching format, titled, "*Principles of Church Life*". Since then, I have not only learnt so much more about the wonders of the church of Christ, I have become even more passionate and convinced about the importance and centrality of the local church in the plan of God.

I have met so many Christians over the years who struggle with "the church" because they see imperfections and lacks. However, the reality is that in this life there will never be perfection (even though the church is better than anything this world has to offer!).

When we adopt this kind of negative attitude about "the

church" we are actually failing to understand that "the church is people" and people are not perfect!

> *If you find the perfect church, don't join it!*
> *Because you'll ruin it!*

The secret I have discovered is not about finding 'the perfect church', but rather, finding 'the church that is perfect for me'!

It is the same with our own natural families. No family is perfect, but my family is 'perfect for me'! The old maxim is helpful; "you can choose your friends but not your family". This is why the Lord Jesus Christ and the apostle Paul were constantly exhorting the believers to "*love one another*"; by overlooking each other's imperfections and lacks.

> *"I therefore, the prisoner in the Lord,*
> *beg you to walk worthy of the calling*
> *with which you were called,*
> *with all lowliness and humility, with patience,*
> ***bearing with one another in love***;
> *being eager to keep the unity of the*
> *Spirit in the bond of peace."*
> *Ephesians 4:1-3*

I found the 'perfect church for me' and it's been a marvelous journey with so many awesome people over the last 54 years.

> *There is no 'perfect church',*
> *only the church that is 'perfect for me'*

I believe it is through the planting of millions of local churches that our world, with all it's ethnicities, cultures and variety, will be able to witness the Gospel of the Lord Jesus Christ being lived out before their very eyes in their own particular community.

> *"Therefore go and make*
> *disciples of all* **NATIONS**
> *(**"ethnos",** G1484, "a tribe,*
> *nation, **people group**")*
> *baptizing them in the name of the Father*
> *and the Son and the Holy Spirit,*
> *teaching them to obey everything*
> *I have commanded you.*
> *And remember, I am with you*
> *always, to the end of the age."*
> *Matthew 28:19-20*

The Revelation of the House of God

Jacob discovered the importance of God's house when he met God in a dream and received the revelation of the house of God. Everything changed for him in that moment because what he knew from information now became what he knew from revelation.

> *"Then Jacob woke up and thought,*
> *"Surely the Lord is in this place,*
> *but I did not realize it!"*
> *He was afraid and said, "What*
> *an awesome place this is!*
> *This is nothing else than the* **HOUSE OF GOD!**
> ***This is the GATE OF HEAVEN!"***
> *Genesis 28:16-17 NET*

There is nothing more important to the Lord Jesus Christ than His Church. The Church holds central place in His affections, purpose and sacrifice at the cross of Calvary.

Yes, Jesus Christ died for you and me personally, but He also had a far bigger idea in mind; Christ died for His people corporately, the church that was to be "*for all ages*" (Ephesians 3:21).

"Christ loves the Church and
gave Himself for her."
Ephesians 5:25

The Church is Christ's Work

Christ's central work on earth today is the establishing and building of His Church. His ultimate mission is to present the church blameless, mature and complete before Himself and the Father at His second coming.

"That He might sanctify and cleanse it
with the washing of water by the word,
That He might present it to
Himself a glorious church,
not having spot, or wrinkle, or any such thing;
but that it should be holy and without blemish."
Ephesians 5:26-27

Therefore, the Lord Jesus Christ measures the sincerity and validity of every Christian, and every Christian endeavour, by their love, commitment and contribution to the establishing, encouragement and building of His people, the Church.

"By this we know love, because
He laid down His life for us.
And we ought to lay down our lives
for the brethren (church)."
1John 3:16

The moment we commit ourselves to make the church of Christ our love and our priority, we are immediately aligned with the love, purpose and work of the Lord Jesus Christ on the earth in this present age, "The Church Age".

It has never been God's will that we should live our faith alone and in isolation, but rather to be vitally connected to and a part of His church family, the House of God.

"Now therefore you are no longer
strangers and foreigners,
but fellow-citizens with the saints,
and of the household of God."
Ephesians 2:19

In the book of Acts, from the beginning of the New Testament Church age, we discover that everyone who believed in the Lord Jesus Christ was "**added to the Church**".

> *"...and the Lord **added to the church***
> *daily those who were being saved"*
> *Acts 2:47*

The moment we are "**born again**" we become part of God's church family, the House of God. Just as we were born naturally into our earthly family, our spiritual new birth experience places us automatically into our spiritual and heavenly family on earth, the house of God.

> *"For this reason I bow my knees to the*
> *Father of our Lord Jesus Christ,*
> *from whom **the whole family in***
> ***heaven and earth is named.***"
> *Ephesians 3:14-15*

This book is written so you might know where you belong and how to belong **IN YOUR LOCAL CHURCH FAMILY, THE HOUSE OF GOD.**

Chapter One

THE CHURCH HAS ALWAYS BEEN GOD'S PLAN

An overview of the Scriptures reveal that the church has always been God's plan and method.

The First Church - The 'Garden of Eden Church'

In the very beginning the Church is revealed as the centre piece of God's plan for mankind.

God had created the world and declared "*It is good*" and then He created mankind and declared, "*It is very good!*"

So the question begs asking; if the created world was 'good' and 'very good', why did God then place Adam and Eve in the Garden of Eden? Wasn't the world already good enough for them to live in?

However, when we understand the idea of the Church we find the answer to this question.

The Garden of Eden was in fact the inauguration by God of the concept of the Church.

In every period of history since the Garden of Eden, God has always established His 'Church', or 'House', and presences Himself in it and works through it to fulfil His divine purpose.

> *"Unto him be glory **in the**
> **church by Christ Jesus**
> **throughout all ages**, world without end. Amen."*
> *Ephesians 3:21*

The 'Church' was established by God to be the central place, or hub, from which His divine blessings, authority and purposes would be revealed.

His Church is where the embodiment of these divine attributes are to be found and from where they would flow out for the blessing and benefit of the whole world.

God chooses the few to bless the many

The central idea of the church is that the 'few', the 'chosen of God', would be the source of blessing to the 'many', the 'called of God'.

> *"To the intent that now unto the principalities*
> *and powers in heavenly places*
> ***might be known by the church the***
> ***manifold wisdom of God,***
> *According to the eternal purpose which*
> *he purposed in Christ Jesus our Lord."*
> *Ephesians 3:10-11*

This is how God has always worked: **God chooses the few to bless the many!**

> *"So God created man in his own image,*
> *in the image of God created he him;*
> *male and female created He them.*
> *And God blessed them, and*
> *God said unto them,*
> *Be fruitful, and multiply, and replenish*
> *the earth, and subdue it:*
> ***and have dominion*** *over the fish of the*
> *sea, and over the fowl of the air,*

and over every living thing that
moves upon the earth."
Genesis 1:27-28

The 'Garden of Eden Church' was the place of relationships

It was in the 'Garden of Eden Church' that God established personal relationship with Adam and Eve.

"And they heard the voice of the Lord God
walking in the garden in the cool of the day…"
Genesis 3:8

This 'Garden of Eden Church' was the haven, the place of retreat and the environment in which relationship with God would occur. The Lord God would come every evening, *"in the cool of the day"*, to walk and commune with Adam and Eve.

God is omnipresent in the world and nature reveals His existence and divine power.

"Because what may be known of
God is manifest in them;

for God has shown it to them.
For since the creation of the world His
invisible attributes are clearly seen,
being understood by the things that are made,
even His eternal power and Godhead;
so that they are without excuse."
Romans 1:19-20

However, it is in the Garden, or the 'Church', that God is personally revealed, known and experienced by Adam and Eve, His people.

Satan and the anti-Church spirit

We also observe the satanic strategy right from the beginning to destroy the church, or House of God, because the blessing of the nations of the world flow from it.

If the Devil could weaken, fracture, or even destroy the church, his mission would be fulfilled and God's eternal purpose thwarted.

However, God is never hindered or vanquished by

anyone, or anything. Nothing can prevent the fulfilling of His divine purpose for His people, the church!

"And it shall come to pass in the last days,
that the mountain of the Lord's house
shall be established in the top of the
mountains, and shall be exalted above the
hills; and all nations shall flow unto it.
And many people shall go and say,
Come, let us go up to the mountain of the Lord,
to the House of the God of Jacob;
and he will teach us of his ways,
and we will walk in his paths:
for out of Zion shall go forth the law, and
the word of the Lord from Jerusalem."
Isaiah 2:2-3

The 'House of God Church' - Jacob's dream in Bethel

According to '*the law of first reference*', where a subject is first mentioned in the Bible, Jacob's dream encounter in Genesis 28 is foundational to our understanding of the church.

It is here at Bethel, the house of God, that Jacob is transformed forever in meeting the God of the House of God.

In this chapter we see the following characteristics revealed to Jacob about the House of God.

First, the House of God, or church, is the **"gate of heaven"**.

> *"How awesome is this place!*
> *This is none other than the House of God,*
> *And this is **the gate of heaven**."*
> *Genesis 28:17*

A gate is simply an opening door or place of entrance by which we can access what is available in the house, and, a place of a closing door that provides security and safety.

The House of God, the church, is where God's blessing, favor, salvation, provision, protection, security and safety are found.

We find all we need when we enter the door of God's House and are joined to the body of Christ where His "*fulness*" resides.

> *"And has put all things under His feet,*
> *and gave Him to be the head over*
> *all things to the **church**,*
> ***Which is His body**,*

the **fulness of Him who fills all in all**."
Ephesians 1:23

The "*fulness*", therefore, is found in the body of Christ, the church, not in the individual Christian.

"**Till WE all come** in the unity of the faith,
and of the knowledge of the Son
of God, unto a perfect man,
unto the measure of the stature
of the **fulness of Christ.**"
Ephesians 3:19 Amplified

No individual Christian can claim that they posses everything they need in themselves and by themselves. The "**fulness**" is "**supplied**" by Christ through the "**joints and ligaments**" of the body of Christ.

Therefore, if we are not joined to, connected and committed in a local church family we are "out of touch" with Christ.

"They're completely out of touch
with the source of life, Christ,
who puts us together in one piece..."

Colossians 2:19 Message Bible
The Church is nourished by "*Joints*" and "*Ligaments*"

The "*joints*" in the body are **two or more members who are joined together by Christ** to function together for a purpose. For example, knee joints are for movement, hand joints are for serving the body.

The "*ligaments"* in the body are the **covenant relationships** and **commitments** we make that "*knit*" us and bind us together in the body of Christ.

> *"and not holding firmly to the Head,*
> ***from whom all the body,***
> ***being supplied and knit together***
> ***through the joints and ligaments***,
> *grows with God's growth."*
> *Colossians 2:19 WEB*

Second, the House of God is **the connection point between heaven and earth**.

In his dream Jacob saw a ladder stretching from earth to heaven. Angels were ascending to God in heaven and descending to the House of God on earth and the Lord stood above it.

It is important to recognize that the first direction and focus of the church is always 'God-ward' ("*ascending*") and then second, reaching out to the world ("*descending*").

> *"And he dreamed and behold,*
> *there was a ladder (margin – "staircase")*
> *set up on the earth,*
> *and the top of it reached to heaven.*
> *And behold, the angels of God*
> *were **ascending** and **descending** on it!*
> *And behold, the Lord stood above it."*
> *Genesis 28:12-13*

Jesus spoke of this connection between heaven and the church in Matthew 16 when He declared that the church would have the authority of heaven on earth.

> *"And I will give to you the keys*
> *of the kingdom of heaven:*
> *and whatever you bind on earth*
> *shall be bound in heaven:*
> *and whatever you loose on earth*
> *shall be loosed in heaven."*
> *Matthew 16:19*

This is the concept of an "*open heaven*" which exists over the local church, or house of God.

> *"If I will not **open the windows**
> **of heaven** for you
> and pour down for you a **blessing**
> that there will **not be room**
> **enough to receive it**."*
> *Malachi 3:10*

An open heaven over the church is discovered when that which is in heaven is found in the church. This is the place of divine favor, blessing and provision. This has always been God's purpose for His church.

> *"Who has blessed us in Christ
> with every spiritual blessing in heavenly places."*
> *Ephesians 1:3*

> *GOD WANTS AN OPEN DOOR OF
> HEAVEN OVER THE CHURCH*
>
> *AND THE CHURCH TO HAVE AN
> OPEN DOOR TO THE WORLD*

It has always been God's intention that His kingdom would come on earth through His people, the church.

The calling of every local church, therefore, is to be connectors between heaven and earth, the spiritual and the natural and the unseen and the seen.

The local church exists to bring God's will and purpose into the earth.

> *"Your kingdom come,*
> *Your will be done ON EARTH*
> *As it is IN HEAVEN"*
> *Matthew 6:10*

Therefore, salvation and all its blessings are found **IN** the church - in His people. Salvation is known, experienced and ministered **THROUGH** the church - through His people. But salvation is not **BY** the church - salvation is by Christ alone!

> *"Now all things are of God,*
> *who has reconciled us to himself*
> *through Jesus Christ,*
> *and has given us the ministry of reconciliation;*
> *that is, that God was in Christ*

> *reconciling the world to himself,*
> *not imputing their trespasses to them,*
> *and has committed to us the*
> *word of reconciliation.*
> *Now then, we are ambassadors for Christ,*
> *as though God were pleading through us:*
> *we implore you on Christ's behalf,*
> *be reconciled to God."*
> *2Corinthians 5:18-20*

Third, the House of God is the place of **the altar of God**.

The first thing that Jacob did in response to his dream and revelation of the house of God was to construct an altar. He immediately sacrificed what he had with him; a flask of oil which he poured as an offering over the altar.

This signified that the house of God is the place of the altar of sacrifice where the presence of God would be revealed.

Jacob's two promises to God

Then Jacob made two promises to God as a result of his revelation.

First, he would bring his 'tithe' (tenth) of all that God would give him to the House of God as an act of worship.

Why did Jacob promise this? Because he now wanted to be a good boy and do what his father Isaac did? Not at all!

Tithing from revelation

Jacob promised to tithe to God as his act of worship in response to the revelation given to him by God! From now on Jacob would live out from his revelation of God and the house of God.

He would no longer live out from his human thinking or desires, or any religious obligation. He was now truly a "*son of Abraham*" because his revelation caused him to live by faith!

> *"just as Abraham believed God,*
> *and it was accounted to him for righteousness.*
> ***Therefore know that only***
> ***those who are of faith,***
> ***are sons of Abraham.*** *"*
> *Galatians 3:6-7*

Building God's House from revelation

Second, Jacob volunteered himself freely to serve God by building the House of God. Again, this decision came from his revelation that the house of God would be his first priority.

> *"And Jacob vowed a vow, saying,*
> *If God will be with me, and will*
> *keep me in this way that I go,*
> *and will give me bread to eat,*
> *and clothes to put on,*
> *So that I come again to my*
> *father's house in peace;*
> *then shall the Lord be my God:*
> *And this stone, which I have set for*
> *a pillar, shall be God's house:*
> *and of all that you shall give me I will*
> *surely give the tenth to You."*
> *Genesis 28:20-22*

The Church is the place of God's Altar

The church, like every house of God from the very beginning of its existence prioritized the establishing of an altar for spiritual sacrifices and the service to God at its core.

> *"You also, as living stones, are being built up*
> *a spiritual house, a holy priesthood,*
> ***to offer up spiritual sacrifices***
> *acceptable to God through Jesus Christ."*
> *Hebrews 13:15*

We are called to be "*royal priests*" and to fulfill our service as ministers of God's House.

As members of the church we are appointed by God to participate, to contribute and to serve in, through and for God's house.

> *Every house of God that ever existed*
> *was built on the same thing;*
> *the altar of sacrifice and service to God*

Therefore, the central position, place and activity in the House of God has always been, and will ever be, the altar of God.

- Every patriarch established an altar
- Every prophet established an altar
- Every tabernacle established an altar
- Every temple established an altar
- Every local church is to establish an altar

This practice of altar ministry was formalized in the tabernacle of Moses when the tribe of Levi was set apart to the priestly office.

In the New Testament nothing changed

There is a spiritual house of God, the church.

> *"You also, as living stones, are being*
> *built up a spiritual house…"*
> *1Peter 2:5*

There is a Melchizedek high priest, the Lord Jesus Christ.

> *"Seeing then that we have a great high priest,*
> *that is passed into the heavens,*
> *Jesus the Son of God,*
> *let us hold fast our profession."*
> *Hebrews 4:14*

There is a priesthood, the believers.

> *"You also are…a holy priesthood"*
> *1Peter 2:5*

There is an altar to minister spiritual sacrifices and offerings

> *"...to offer up spiritual sacrifices, acceptable*
> *to God through Jesus Christ."*
> *1Peter 2:5*

Every local church is to establish an altar

Therefore, every local church is appointed by God to establish an altar. This is the first and most important priority of every church.

Some church traditions believe that the establishing of a table to celebrate communion is the priority. While some believe that the establishing of a pulpit for preaching the Gospel is the priority. In modern times some churches believe in the establishing of a charity to minister to the poor and needy is the priority.

However, although communion, preaching and charity, for example, are important, they are secondary to the establishing of an altar in the House of God!

The altar is central to church life

The local church is where the altar of God is central to it's life and activity. This is because the local church was ordained by God to be a house of sacrifice and service to Him.

Therefore, all other activities should flow from and out of the 'altar ministry' in the church, the House of God.

The altar is foundational for all service and ministry

The altar is the foundation of all service and ministry to and for God because by its very nature the altar is a place of sacrifice, death, denial and surrender.

Sacrifice is the act of worship in which we lay down our lives, agendas and desires in complete surrender and commitment to God. This is the beginning and foundation of all true ministry and service to God.

Serving out of Revelation

Our motive to serve, give or minister is not because we

are religiously obligated to, or that we even enjoy service. Rather, we are to serve out from a revelation of divine ownership which causes a response of sacrifice to Christ. This is our *"spiritual worship"*.

> *"I appeal to you therefore, brothers,*
> *to present your bodies as a*
> ***living sacrifice to God,***
> *which is your **spiritual worship**."*
> *Rom 12:1*

The Altar in the New Testament

The New Testament continued this concept of 'altar ministry' beginning with Jesus' declaration that God's house is to be a "house of prayer".

> *"My House shall be called a*
> *HOUSE OF PRAYER."*
> *Matthew 21:13*

This declaration by Jesus clearly identified the priority for every church; the altar of the seeking of God in prayer.

This is evidenced when the following 'altar ministries' are prioritized in church life:-

1. Praise

*"Through Him then let us continually
offer up a SACRIFICE OF PRAISE to God,
that is, the fruit of our lips."*
Hebrews 13:15

2. Worship

*"Therefore, let us be grateful
for receiving a kingdom
that cannot be shaken, and let us
OFFER TO GOD ACCEPTABLE WORSHIP
with reverence and awe."*
Hebrews 12:28

3. Giving of Tithes and Offerings

*"Bring all the TITHES into the STOREHOUSE,
that there may be food in MY HOUSE."*
Malachi 3:10

*"Do you not know that those who are employed
in the temple service get their
food from the temple,
and those who SERVE AT THE ALTAR
SHARE IN THE SACRIFICIAL OFFERINGS?
IN THE SAME WAY,
THE LORD HAS COMMANDED
That those who preach the Gospel
SHOULD GET THEIR LIVING BY THE GOSPEL."
1Corinthians 9:13-14*

4. Service and Ministry

*"Even if I were to be poured out as a
DRINK OFFERING upon the
SACRIFICIAL OFFERING OF YOUR FAITH,
I am glad and rejoice with you all."
Philippians 2:17*

5. Doing Good and meeting needs

*"Do not neglect to do good and
to share what you have,
for with such SACRIFICES are pleasing to God."
Hebrews 13:16*

*"You will be ENRICHED IN EVERY WAY
to be GENEROUS IN EVERY WAY."
2Corinthians 9:11*

Fourth, the house of God is **to establish, equip and release the "priesthood of believers".**

Every member of the church is called by God to function as a priest with the priority of offering spiritual sacrifices to God. This is to occur '**in**' the House of God (the church 'gathered') and '**through**' the church (the church 'scattered').

*"You yourselves like living stones
are being built up as a SPIRITUAL HOUSE,
to be a HOLY PRIESTHOOD,
to offer spiritual sacrifices acceptable to God."
1Peter 2:5*

Every believer is a priest

The leaders and pastors are not the only priests in the church. Every believer is a priest, functioning as the "body of Christ".

"It was He who gave some as
apostles, some as prophets,
some as evangelists, and some
as pastors and teachers,
to equip the saints for the work of ministry,
that is, to build up the body of Christ."
Ephesians 4:11-12 NET

This "*work of ministry*" by the "*saints*", or believers, is to serve God as priests in and through the local church.

With this purpose in mind, God places, gifts and anoints every believer with a part to play to "*build up the body of Christ*".

"Even so you, since you are
zealous for spiritual gifts,
let it be for the edification (building up)
of the church that you seek to excel."
1Corinthians 14:12

It is every leaders job "*to equip the saints for the work of ministry.*" Therefore, the leaders are to:

"fully equip and perfect the saints (God's people)", that is, to identify, train and mobilize every believer to participate in the building up and "edification" of the church. These are the "works of service" the apostle Paul described in Ephesians 4:12 (Amplified Bible)

Priesthood begins at the point of sacrifice not service

Our ministry to God as priests begins at the point of sacrifice not service. Our primary calling is to be priests to God, not a leader, not a preacher or prophet. These follow second. This understanding comes from a revelation of the supremacy of the altar of God.

> *"All work for God begins with consecration or is based on surrender. But such consecration or surrender only comes through revelation."*
> *(Watchman Nee, "God's Work")*

In other words, our primary calling is to be disciples and priests first, offering gifts and sacrifices to God. We are to be leaders and ministers second.

"Every high priest is appointed
to OFFER GIFTS AND SACRIFICES."
Hebrews 8:3

In the New Testament we discover that these *"spiritual sacrifices"* are the *"gifts and sacrifices"* we are to offer to God on the altar in God's house, the local church.

The first gift to God - ourselves

The presenting of ourselves to God as *"living sacrifices"* on the altar of God's House is the very first gift we are to give to God.

"I appeal to you therefore, brothers,
to present your bodies as a
living sacrifice to God,
which is your spiritual worship."
Rom 12:1

This is the sacrifice of our whole self to God without reservation, time limit or condition. Our hearts, our minds, our bodies, our lives, our talents, our time, our treasure, our all!

God wants everything on the altar

Someone once complained to me saying, "all the church wants is our money!" To which I instantly responded, "Please don't sell us short! God wants more than our money, He wants everything! Our hearts, our lives, our time, our talents, our marriages, our careers, EVERYTHING!"

The altar claims all

A sacrificial lamb doesn't 'half die' on the altar! Nor does a sacrificial lamb change it's mind half way through the sacrificial ceremony to get off the altar! It is the nature of the altar to claim everything!

Knowing Jesus as Saviour AND Lord

It is so important to understand that Jesus didn't just save us FROM our sin, He saved us TO His divine lordship. The new life that Christ offers cannot be lived apart from his Lordship of our lives.

> *If Jesus isn't Lord of all,*
> *then He isn't Lord at all!*

It is only when we truly understand this concept of sacrifice, the altar claiming all, that we will be completely yielded and presented to God forever with no reservation. This is what it means to be a "*living sacrifice*".

As "living sacrifices" we are called to serve God sacrificially, alive, enthusiastically and full of vigor!

> *"Never lagging behind in diligence;*
> *aglow in the Spirit,*
> *enthusiastically serving the Lord."*
> *Romans 12:11 Amplified Bible*

The second gift to God - service to others

We are called to present our service, or ministry, as priests for the benefit and edification of the House of God. This is because we no longer belong to ourselves.

We belong to God and now we serve God as priests for the benefit, building up, edification and the betterment of others.

> *"…to equip the saints FOR THE*
> *WORK OF MINISTRY,*
> *for BUILDING UP the Body of Christ…"*
> *Ephesians 4:12*

The 'Ark Church'

When God instructed Noah to build the ark, he was not just building a boat. Noah was building an 'Ark Church'; a place of blessing, protection and provision for a new world in which the righteousness of faith would exist.

> *"By faith Noah, being warned of*
> *God of things not seen as yet,*
> *moved with fear, prepared an ark*
> *to the saving of his house;*
> *by the which he condemned the world,*
> *and became heir of the righteousness*
> *which is by faith."*
> *Hebrews 11:7*

Here we see the purpose of the church in providing a place of blessing, protection and provision for the family of God; a 'new world' from God based on the "*righteousness of faith*".

> *"For therein is the **righteousness of**
> ***God** revealed from faith to faith:*
> *as it is written, **The just shall live by faith**."*
> *Romans 1:17*

The Church in the Wilderness - The Children of Israel

The Children of Israel were called by God to be His special people. Here we see the purpose of God to call His people to Himself.

> *"This is He, that was in **the***
> ***church in the wilderness***
> *with the angel which spake to*
> *him in the mount Sinai,*
> *and with our fathers: who received the*
> *lively oracles to give unto us."*
> *Acts 7:38*

The apostle Paul presented the calling of Israel as an example for us.

> *"Now these things became our examples,*
> *to the intent that we should not lust*
> *after evil things as they also lusted."*
> *1Corinthians 10:6*

Just like Israel, we are to fulfill the purpose of God to be a blessing to the many (the world) through the few (the church).

"For you are a holy people
unto the Lord your God:
the Lord your God has chosen you to
be a special people unto Himself,
above all people that are upon
the face of the earth.
The Lord did not set His love
upon you, nor choose you,
because you were more in
number than any people;
for you were the fewest of all people."
Deuteronomy 7:6-8

The Eternal Universal Church in Heaven

The ultimate expression of the church will be seen at the second coming of Christ . The church will not end, but rather, she will be raised with Christ in heaven, glorified and perfected, seated at His right hand, ruling and reigning with Christ in all His glory for ever and ever!

"That he might present it to
himself a glorious church,
not having spot, or wrinkle, or any such thing;
but that it should be holy and without blemish."
Ephesians 5:27

This will be the **PERFECT, GLORIOUS CHURCH**, resurrected and glorified for eternity by the power of God.

"And I saw a new heaven and a new earth:
for the first heaven and the first earth were
passed away; and there was no more sea.
And I John saw the holy city, new Jerusalem,
coming down from God out of heaven,
prepared as a bride adorned for her husband.
And I heard a great voice out of heaven saying,
Behold, the tabernacle of God is with men,
and he will dwell with them, and
they shall be his people,
and God himself shall be with
them, and be their God."
Revelation 21:1-3

Chapter Two

THE PURPOSE OF THE CHURCH

Why is the church so important? What's the big deal about it?

Many would exclaim, "I don't have to go to church to be a Christian!" Which of course, is a totally incorrect understanding of the very nature of the church.

This is because 'being a Christian' is not about 'GOING' to church, the building, or 'GOING' to a meeting, an activity - **THE PEOPLE OF GOD ARE THE CHURCH**!

'Church' is all about '**BEING THE CHURCH'** not about 'doing church', or 'going to church'!

This is why the Lord added the new believers from the very beginning to the church.

*"And **the Lord added to the church***
daily those who were being saved."
Acts 2:47

Our calling, therefore, is to be joined as active members into the body of Christ, the Church, and to live our life of faith in and through the community of the local church.

"And let the peace of God rule in your hearts,
to which also you were called in one body;
and be thankful."
Colossians 3:15

However, once we understand the purpose of the church we will not only appreciate this great gift of God's grace to us, we will want to be involved, contribute and be a part of our local church family.

What then are the purposes of the church?

The four central purposes of the church

EXALTATION - the church exists for the pleasure, satisfaction and glory of God

The church was created by God for His own pleasure, satisfaction and glory. So the church exists to live for the "*good pleasure of His will*" and in so doing brings great satisfaction and joy to God.

> *"Having predestinated us unto the adoption*
> *of children by Jesus Christ to Himself,*
> ***according to the good pleasure of his will***,
> *To the praise of the glory of his grace,*
> *wherein He has made us*
> *accepted in the beloved."*
> *Ephesians 1:5-6*

'The world', on the other hand, lives ignorantly or knowingly, in opposition to God, even though He loves them and gave His only son for them. In so doing they bring much pain and disappointment to His heart. God has chosen the church to be His ambassadors inviting all to believe in Christ and become part of His church family and enjoy the benefits of His eternal love, grace and blessings.

EVANGELISM - the church exists to preach the Gospel of Christ to win lost people and make disciples

From the very beginning of the church at the ascension of

Christ, a clear and specific command was given by Jesus Christ as to His main purpose for the church.

This is called "**THE GREAT COMMISSION**" and is recorded in Matthew and Mark and recalled later by Luke in the Acts of the Apostles.

"And Jesus came and spake unto them, saying,
All power is given unto me in
heaven and in earth.
Go therefore, and teach all nations,
baptizing them in the name of the Father,
and of the Son, and of the Holy Spirit:
Teaching them to observe all things
whatsoever I have commanded you:
and, lo, I am with you always, even
unto the end of the world. Amen."
Matthew 28:18-20

"And he said unto them,
Go into all the world, and preach
the gospel to every creature.
He who believes and is baptized shall be saved;
but he who does not believe shall be damned.
And these signs shall follow them that believe;
In my name shall they cast out devils;

they shall speak with new tongues;
They shall take up serpents; and if they drink any
deadly thing, it shall not hurt them; they shall
lay hands on the sick, and they shall recover."
Mark 16:15-18

"And he said unto them, It is not for you
to know the times or the seasons,
which the Father has put in His own power.
But you shall receive power, after the
Holy Spirit has come upon you:
and you shall be witnesses unto me
both in Jerusalem, and in all Judaea,
and in Samaria, and unto the
uttermost part of the earth."
Acts 1:7-8

The "Great Commission" can be summarized from Matthew 28 and Mark 16 as follows:-

"**GO"** - be active, proactive and out reaching to lost people

"**BE WITNESSES TO ME**" - by spirit empowered lives showing Christ and His abundant life through our lives

"**PREACH THE GOSPEL**" - declaring and communicating the good news that "*Christ died for our sins, He was buried, He rose again...*" (1Corinthians 15:1-9)

"**TO EVERY CREATURE...ALL THE NATIONS**" - to every 'ethnic (people group) on the earth

"**MAKE DISCIPLES**" - "*Teaching them to obey My commands*"

"**THESE SIGNS WILL FOLLOW**" - 'supernatural evangelism' resulting in miraculous new birth conversions, signs and wonders

And they simply went out and obeyed!

> *"And they went out, and preached every where,*
> *the Lord working with them,*
> *and confirming the word with*
> *accompanying signs. Amen"*
> *Mark 16:20*

In my book on lifestyle evangelism, "**Tell Your Story**", I dedicate a whole chapter entitled "**Evangelism and Your Church**" (chapter 9), which outlines the need for the centrality of evangelism in the local church:-

"The local church is called to obey the Great Commission

When the Great Commission is placed front and centre in a local church's vision, purpose and activity "**we will create an environment and culture that welcomes and includes the unchurched, just like our Lord Jesus Christ": "I came not to call the righteous, but sinners to repentance**.

Church for the Unchurched

Therefore, building and focusing the local church around the attraction of the unchurched (evangelism) and the establishing of New Christians (discipleship) is the core mission of the church.

When every pastor, leader and member of our churches recognizes that "our church doesn't exist for me, our church exists for the unchurched, the lost, those who haven't discovered Jesus yet", we will experience effective evangelism like we've never seen before!"

> *"AS LONG AS ONE PERSON*
> *IN OUR COMMUNITY*
> *DOESN'T KNOW THE LORD,*
> *WE'RE OPEN FOR BUSINESS!"*
>
> *("Tell Your Story", chapter 9)*

EDIFICATION - the church exists to disciple, build up and strengthen believers

'Becoming a Christian' is not about the 'Christianization' of our lives in order to improve our lives and become members of a church community.

Rather, 'becoming a Christian' is about the 'Discipleship' of our lives in which we under go radical transformation into becoming a follower of the Lord Jesus Christ!

This idea of 'being Christianized' has continued throughout western cultures to the present day.

For example, most Australians (86% - National Church Life Survey, Australia) believe in God, and will claim that they are Christians. However, less than 5% are actually committed to a church and a Christian lifestyle!

Therefore, a 'Christian' is often seen as a person who:-

1. Goes to church
2. Lives by the 'golden rule'
3. Dresses in conservative, 'Christian Culture' clothing
4. Reads their Bible and prays
5. Doesn't drink alcohol, smoke or swear
6. Lives a 'moral' and narrow life
7. Votes for right wing politicians
8. Is generally regarded as 'nerdy'

However, the Bible teaches that being a disciple of Christ is more about WHO we are than WHAT we do!

> *"Therefore, if anyone is in Christ,*
> *he is a new creation,*
> *old things have passed away, and*
> *look, all things are new."*
> *2Corinthians 5:17*

EXPANSION - the church exists to increase and grow the influence of the kingdom of God in the world

The central ways in which the local church expands the kingdom of God in the earth is through soul winning and discipling believers. This is accelerated when leaders are raised in the local church because leaders multiply soul winning and disciple making!

"WIN LOST PEOPLE
MAKE DISCIPLES
GROW LEADERS"

Church planting is the most effective way to achieve the purpose of expansion. This is because once a local church is established it contains all the resources within itself to expand the kingdom of God by itself.

This is the vision of the local church: a 'self contained' church planting, kingdom expanding community of faith.

"And I say to you, That you are Peter,
and upon this rock I will build my church;
and the gates of hell shall not prevail against it.
And I will give unto thee the keys
of the kingdom of heaven:
and whatsoever thou shalt bind on earth shall
be bound in heaven: and whatsoever thou shalt
loose on earth shall be loosed in heaven."
Matthew 16:18-19

Chapter Three

PICTURES OF THE CHURCH

The Scriptures use many pictures to convey and illustrate the various aspects and characteristics of the local church.

THE FAMILY OF GOD

The most common picture and language used in the Scriptures to illustrate the church would be the family of God.

> *"For this cause I bow my knees unto*
> *the Father of our Lord Jesus Christ,*
> *from whom the whole family in*
> *heaven and earth is named."*
> *Ephesians 3:14-25*

God has chosen to reveal Himself to us as our loving, heavenly father and we are His children. This reveals the nature of God and His primary desire to be in relationship with us.

Membership of God's family

In a natural family membership is by **birth** or **adoption**. The Scriptures use these two analogies to show how we are made members of the family of God.

The New Birth

Being 'born again' is the essential Biblical experience that initiates membership into the family of God. To be part of God's family we must be able to participate in God's family life, which is both spiritual and supernatural.

Therefore, we must be born again, or "*from above*" (Bible margin), spiritually and supernaturally to be made compatible and to be able to participate effectively in God's family.

*"Jesus answered and said unto
him, Truly, truly, I say to you,
Except a man is born again, he
cannot **see** the kingdom of God.
Except a man be born of water and of the Spirit,
he cannot **enter** into the kingdom of God.
That which is born of the flesh is flesh;
and that which is born of the Spirit is **spirit**."
John 3:3,5-6*

The moment we are born again in the Spirit we carry the divine nature of God within us.

*"Whereby are given to us exceeding
great and precious promises:
that by these you might be **partakers
of the divine nature**,
having escaped the corruption that
is in the world through lust."
2Peter 1:4*

The Adoption as Children

The concept of adoption is also used in the Scriptures. It shows us how we are members of God's family by having a legal standing with God with the full heir rights and privileges as a son or daughter of God.

"For you have not received the spirit
of bondage again to fear;
*but you have received the **Spirit of***
***adoption**, whereby we cry, Abba, Father.*
The Spirit itself bears witness with our
spirit, that we are the children of God:
*And if children, **then heirs; heirs of***
***God, and joint-heirs with Christ**…"*
Romans 8:15-17

THE BODY OF CHRIST

The picture of the local church as Christ's body illustrates the wonderful and intimate connection of the relationship between Christ, as the Head of the body, and the saints who are the members of Christ's body.

The Head of the Body

The Lord Jesus Christ is the head of the body. From Christ flows all the life, guidance, direction, health and initiation to the body.

"And has put all things under His feet,
*and gave Him to be **the head over***
all things to the church,
***Which is his body**, the fulness*
of him that fills all in all."
Ephesians 1:22-23

The Lord Jesus Christ being the head of the body, the church, means the following:-

First, the head of the body is the **centre of authority**.

"Wives, submit yourselves unto your
own husbands, as unto the Lord.
For the husband is the head of the wife,
even as Christ is the head of the church:
and he is the savior of the body.
Therefore as the church is subject unto Christ,
so let the wives be to their own
husbands in every thing.
This is a great mystery,
but I speak concerning Christ and the church."
Ephesians 22-24, 32

Second, the head of the body is the **coordination centre**.

> *"And not holding fast to the **Head**,*
> ***from whom** all the body,*
> *nourished and knit together by*
> *joints and ligaments,*
> *grows with the increase that is from God."*
> *Colossians 2:19*

Third, the head of the body is the **nerve centre**.

Every part of the body is connected by an elaborate nervous system. The human brain registers and directs everything that is happening in the body through the nervous system.

The apostle Paul understood this concept when he wrote:-

> *"That there should be no schism in the body;*
> *but that the members should have*
> *the same care one for another.*
> *And whether one member suffer,*
> *all the members suffer with it;*
> *or one member be honored, all*
> *the members rejoice with it.*
> *Now you are the body of Christ,*

> *and members in particular."*
> *1Corinthians 12:25-27*

It is through this vital connection with Christ as the head of the church and all the members that the whole body begins to flow in 'body life'.

The Members of the Body

The members of the body of Christ, the local church, are to embody the following six important things that the apostle Paul explained in Corinthians and Romans:-

First, **every member has a set place**.

> *"But now God has set the*
> *members, each one of them,*
> *in the body just as He pleased."*
> *1Corinthians 12:18*

Second, **every member is important**.

> *"But now indeed there are many*
> *members, yet one body.*

And the eye cannot say to the hand,
"I have no need of you";
nor again the head to the feet,
"I have no need of you"."
1Corinthians 12:20-21

Third, **every member is different.**

"For as we have many members in one body,
and all members have not the same office:
So we, being many, are one body in Christ,
and every one members one of another.
Having then gifts differing according
to the grace that is given to us..."
Romans 12:4-6

Fourth, **every member has a function.**

"But the manifestation of the Spirit is
given to each one for the profit of all."
1Corinthians 12:7

Fifth, **every member should love, accept and appreciate the other members**.

"That there should be no schism in the body;
but that the members should have
the same care one for another."
1Corinthians 12:25

Sixth, **Christ's distribution of gifts is His delegation of authority.**

The distribution of gifts by Christ to members of His body reveals His delegation of authority.

In other words, the gifts are given to provide an 'order of function' in the body where certain members have 'more authority' than others.

For example, the apostle is "*first*" in the order of function and is to exercise authority over the other gifts such as prophets and teachers.

"And God has appointed these in the church,
***first** apostles, **second** prophets, **third** teachers,*
***after that** miracles, **then** gifts of healings,*
helps, administrations, varieties of tongues."
1Corinthians 12:28

Every gift is accompanied with a different measure, or level, of grace and faith. Grace is the 'right to act' and faith is the 'ability to act'.

> *"For I say, through the grace given to*
> *me, to everyone who is among you,*
> *not to think of himself more highly*
> *than he ought to think;*
> *but to think soberly, as **God has dealt***
> ***to each one a measure of faith.***
> *For as we have many members in one body,*
> *and all members have not the same function,*
> *So we, being many, are one body in Christ,*
> *and individually members of one another.*
> ***Having then gifts differing according***
> ***to the grace that is given to us..."***

THE TEMPLE OF GOD

Throughout the Bible, and especially in the history of Israel, God has always sought for a dwelling place among His people.

For example, the Lord commanded Moses to build a dwelling place so He could dwell there among His people.

> *"And let them make me a sanctuary;*
> *that I may dwell among them."*
> *Exodus 25:8*

God is dwelling in His people

Today, in the church age, God is not dwelling in a physical temple made with hands, He is dwelling in His people, the church.

> *"…for you are the temple of the living God;*
> *as God has said, I will dwell in*
> *them, and walk in them;*
> *and I will be their God, and they*
> *shall be my people."*
> *2Corinthians 6:16*

In this picture of the church, we see that the individual members of the church are "*living stones*" being prepared and built into a temple by God through the Holy Spirit.

> *"You also, **as living stones, are being***
> ***built up a spiritual house**,*
> *a holy priesthood, to offer up spiritual sacrifices*
> *acceptable to God through Jesus Christ."*
> *1Peter 2:5*

This is a work in progress as the local church grows, fits together and develops over time.

"having been built on the foundation
of the apostles and prophets,
Jesus Christ Himself being the chief cornerstone,
in whom the whole building,
being fitted together,
grows into a holy temple in the Lord:
In whom you also are being built together
for a dwelling place of God in the Spirit."
Ephesians 2:20-22

The holy priesthood

This picture of the church shows us that not only are we the 'living building' in which God dwells, we are also the '*holy priesthood*' called to worship and serve God. We are the '*laborers*' working together with God to build His temple.

"For we are God's fellow workers;
you are God's field, you are God's building.
According to the grace of God
which was given unto me,
as a wise master builder I have laid the

foundation, and another builds upon it.
But let each one take heed how he builds on it."
1Corinthians 3:9-10

THE VINEYARD OF GOD

Another common picture and theme of the church throughout the Scriptures is that the people of God are likened to His vineyard, or garden. As such they exist to "*bring forth fruit*" for God's pleasure and glory.

Jesus used this analogy to show the vital connection between Himself and the church and our heavenly father. We also see in this picture the absolute trust and dependency needed by the church to bear fruit.

"I am the true vine, and my
Father is the vinedresser.
Every branch in me that does not
bear fruit He takes away:
and every branch that bears fruit, He
prunes, that it may bear more fruit.
You are already clean because of the
word which I have spoken to you.
Abide in me, and I in you. As the
branch cannot bear fruit of itself,

unless it abides in the vine, neither
can you, unless you abide in Me.
I am the vine, you are the branches.
He who abides in Me, and I in
him, bears much fruit:
for without Me you can do nothing."
John 15:1-5

The 'fruits' of the church

It is clear from the teachings of Jesus and the apostles that true disciples of Jesus Christ produce "*Fruit unto God*". These '*fruits*' include:-

- The fruit of the Spirit - Galatians 5:22-23

- The peaceable fruit of righteousness - James 3:17-18

- The fruit (or harvest) of souls - Luke 10:2

- The fruit of good works - Colossians 1:10

- The fruit of our lips (praise) - Hebrews 13:15

- The fruit of financial prosperity - 2Corinthians 9:10

The Church is to Grow

> *"I planted, Apollos watered, **but God [all the while] was causing the growth**.*
> *So neither is the one who plants nor the one who waters anything,*
> ***but [only] God who causes the growth.***"
> *1Corinthians 3:6-7 Amplified Bible*

Jesus declared to His disciples that His father was glorified when they produced "*much fruit*". Furthermore, God uses the process of pruning to increase fruitfulness in His children.

The church grows in two ways: in 'Quality' and in 'Quantity'.

However, it is not uncommon to observe different church traditions leaning towards one or the other kinds of growth depending on their theology.

For example, groups that believe in the 'smallness' of the church can tend to emphasize 'quality growth', while groups who believe in the 'largeness' of the church can tend to emphasize 'quantity growth'

'Quality Growth' and 'Quantity Growth' are to be held in balance

As in nature, both 'quality growth' and 'quantity growth' are held in balance.

For example, if there is too much 'quality', yields will be low, and a poor harvest will be the result. If there is too much 'quantity' much of the yields will be unusable and resulting in a poor harvest, again.

The secret is in the balance. The ideal harvest is when both quality and quantity are high. However, in the real world of seasonal fluctuations this balance is rarely experienced.

'Quality Growth' and 'Quantity Growth' together produce health

For a local church to experience health there must be a balance between 'Quality Growth' and 'Quantity Growth'.

'**Quality Growth**' refers to the **type** of fruit grown. It is the 'internal growth' of the church, producing the nature and character of God, known as the "***fruit of the Spirit***" (Galatians 5:22-23). This is the 'Disciple Making factor'.

'**Quantity Growth**' refers the **amount** of fruit grown. It is the 'external growth' of the church, producing the numerical growth of new members through conversions, known as the "***fruit of souls***". This is the 'evangelism factor'.

THE FLOCK OF GOD

Throughout the Scriptures God's people are most frequently referred to as His "*Sheep*"and "*Flock*". This picture reveals God's loving care, protection and guidance for His people.

> *"The Lord is my shepherd; I shall not want.*
> *He makes me to lie down in green pastures:*
> *he leads me beside the still*
> *waters. He restores my soul:*
> *he leads me in the paths of*
> *righteousness for his name's sake."*
> *Psalm 23:1-3*

The Lord Jesus referred to Himself as the "*Good Shepherd*" who gives His live for His sheep.

> *"I am the good shepherd:*
> *the good shepherd giveth his life for the sheep."*
> *John 10:11*

The importance of Shepherds

The Lord Jesus challenged Peter about his responsibility as a leader to pastor, or shepherd, His people. By doing this, Peter would prove his love for Jesus.

> *"So when they had dined, Jesus*
> *said to Simon Peter,*
> *Simon, son of Jonas, do you*
> *love me more than these?*
> *He said to Him, Yes, Lord; you*
> *know that I love You.*
> *He said to him, Feed my lambs.*
> *He said to him again the second time,*
> *Simon, son of Jonas, do you love me?*
> *He said to Him, Yes, Lord;*
> *You know that I love You.*
> *He said to him, Feed my sheep.*
> *He said to him the third time, Simon,*
> *son of Jonas, do you love me?*
> *Peter was grieved because he said to*
> *him the third time, Do you love me?*

*And he said to Him, Lord, You know all
things; You know that I love you.
Jesus said to him, Feed my sheep."
John 21:15-17*

The need for Shepherds

The Scriptures reveal the following characteristics of sheep.

First, **sheep go astray**. If sheep are left to their own devices they will tend to wander and go astray. This is why God has always set up pastors over His flock to ensure that His people are not left to "*wander*".

*"My sheep wandered through all the
mountains, and upon every high hill:
yes, my flock was scattered upon
all the face of the earth,
and no one did search or seek after them.
For thus says the Lord God;
Behold, I, even I, will both search for
my sheep, and seek them out.
As a shepherd seeks out his flock in the day
that he is among his sheep that are
scattered; so will I seek out my sheep,
and will deliver them out of all places*

> *where they have been scattered*
> *in the cloudy and dark day."*
> *Ezekiel 34:6,11-12*

Second, **sheep are vulnerable**. Sheep by nature are gentle and as such are the most vulnerable to preying animals. The Scriptures liken God's people to sheep in that they are vulnerable to error, thieves, wolves and hirelings. This is especially true of the young.

It is the responsibility of pastors to protect the flock of God from it's enemies.

Third, **sheep scatter easily**. The experienced shepherd gathers his sheep gently, avoiding all sudden movements or loud noises that could excite or startle the sheep and scatter them.

Jesus' desire was to gather His sheep into His "fold", the church, so they would be safe and together.

> *"And other sheep I have, which are not*
> *of this fold: them also I must bring,*
> *and they shall hear my voice; and there*
> *shall be one fold, and one shepherd."*
> *John 10:16*

Fourth, **sheep need care and tending**. If sheep are not

cared for their wool will grow ragged, uneven and very oily.Through shearing, drenching and regular care, sheep grow quality wool and are kept healthy from parasites and disease.

This is why the pastors of God's people are to keep the welfare of the sheep as the highest priority, so they will not be lacking any good thing.

> *"And I will set up shepherds over*
> *them who will feed them:*
> *and they shall fear no more, nor be dismayed,*
> *neither shall they be lacking, says the Lord."*
> *Jeremiah 23:4*

Pastors are to care for God's flock just as the "*Good Shepherd*" does!

> *"He shall feed His flock like a shepherd:*
> *He shall gather the lambs with His*
> *arm, and carry them in His bosom,*
> *and shall gently lead those that are with young."*
> *Isaiah 40:11*

THE CITY OF GOD

The church is 'God's City' on earth, foreshadowing the glorious "*heavenly Jerusalem*" city that will be revealed in the "*Day of the Lord*". The saints find their citizenship and membership of God's family in her.

"Now, therefore, you are no longer
strangers and foreigners,
but fellow citizens with the saints, and
members of the household of God."
Ephesians 2:19

The writer of Hebrews explains the nature of this great city of God in more detail.

"But you have come to Mount Zion
*and **to the city of the living God,***
***the heavenly Jerusalem**,*
to an innumerable company of angels,
to the general assembly and church of the
firstborn, who are registered in heaven,
to God the Judge of all, to the spirits
of just men made perfect,
to Jesus the mediator of the new covenant,
and to the blood of sprinkling
that speaks better things than that of Abel."
Hebrews 12:22-24

The local church is the visible, tangible and connectable "city of God"

The Lord Jesus declared His people on earth to be a "*city on a hill*". An unmistakable and clear light to show the way to God for all people.

> *"You are the light of the world. A city*
> *that is set on an hill cannot be hid."*
> *Matthew 5:14*

The local church is a lighthouse

The local church is a lighthouse declaring and showing the way of salvation to those in darkness.

> *"For it is God who commanded*
> *light to shine out of darkness,*
> *who has shone in our hearts,*
> *to give the light of the knowledge*
> *of the glory of God*
> *in the face of Jesus Christ."*
> *2Corinthians 4:6*

The apostle Paul described this concept of the church being a visible guide as an "*epistle, known and read by all men*".

> *"You are our epistle written in our hearts,*
> *known and read of all men."*
> *2Corinthians 2:3*

The church is big enough for everyone

John refers to the New Jerusalem as a massive 'cube shaped city'

> *"And I, John, saw the holy city, New Jerusalem,*
> *coming down out of heaven from God...*
> *And the city is laid out as a square, it's*
> *length is as great as it's breadth.*
> *And he measured the city with the*
> *reed: twelve thousand furlongs.*
> *It's length, breadth and the height are equal."*
> *Revelation 21:2,16-17*

The measurements of the city are massive. Imagine this; converting, 12,000 square furlongs to square kilometers, the footprint of the city, is 2,414 square kilometers!

In Australian terms, the base of the holy city stretches approximately from Weipa, Queensland, to Melbourne, Victoria, and squared off to the Western Australian border to Lake Hopkins, WA!

So that is a city as big as all of Queensland, New South Wales, Victoria, South Australia and the Northern Territory!

But the holy city is cubed with the same height… MASSIVE!! No other city is this big or high! The tallest building in the world in Dubai is 848 meters…the holy city is 2,414 kilometers high!

Why?

Because there's room enough in God's heart for everyone!

The tragedy is that many people will continue to reject God's offer of eternal life.

> *"For God so loved the world, that*
> *he gave His only begotten Son,*
> *that whoever believes in Him should not*
> *perish, but have everlasting life."*
> *John 3:16*

Chapter Four

WHAT CONSTITUTES A LOCAL CHURCH?

The word "church" comes from the Greek word "*ekklesia*" (G1577), literally meaning "**called out ones**" and is variously translated "**church**", "**assembly**" and "**congregation**" in the New Testament.

"*Assembly*" means to assemble and "*congregation*" means to congregate. Put simply, the church is meant to be together!

Both in the original Greek language the word "*ekklesia*" was used to define a political assembly of citizens of the ancient Greek city states; "*a gathering of those summoned"* (*Britannica*).

The most common usage of the word "*ekklessia*" in the Scriptures refers to the people of God. In the New

Testament and historically it refers to God's people who have been called out of the world to follow Jesus Christ as a congregation, or assembly, in a given location.

Over the centuries, through translation into other languages and traditions, the word church has also come to mean a physical place where Christians gather for worship.

However, this is not the original New Testament usage and meaning. During the Roman Empire occupation period of 5 BC to 314AD, where Christianity began, it was unlawful and uncommon for Christians to own buildings. This all changed after 314AD when Constantine became Roman emperor following which he converted to Christianity and became a sponsor of the church.

With the rise of the Christianized Europeans the word 'church' came to mean a building or organization, rather than a local congregation of people.

For example, the English word "*church*" comes from the Dutch word "*kerk*" *and* the German word "*kirche*. These words predominantly arose from the catholic and reformed traditions to literally mean 'the *Lord's house*', a physical building, usually in the town centre.

However, many 'non-conformist' Christian groups, for

example, like the Pietists and the Quakers, for example, reacted to this concept and referred to the **people as the church** and the church building, or facility, as a **place of worship**.

Should churches own buildings?

So the question frequently asked is, "should churches own buildings?" Unequivocally, YES! This is in order to facilitate the ministry and work of the church to their local community.

The Church is 'called out to Christ'

The concept of the church originally found it's meaning when God called the children of Israel out of Egypt and slavery. God's purpose was to gather His people to serve Him as His own chosen people.

> *"And you shall say to him, The Lord*
> *God of the Hebrews has sent me to*
> *you, saying, Let my people go, that they*
> *may serve me in the wilderness."*
> *Ex 7:16*

The Church is called 'outside the Camp'

The writer of the Epistle of Hebrews encourages believers to hear the call of God and go to Christ "*outside the camp*", or the world.

> *"Therefore Jesus also,*
> *that He might sanctify the people*
> *through His own blood,*
> *suffered **outside of the gate**.*
> *Let us therefore **go out to Him outside**
> **of the camp**, bearing His reproach.*
> *For we don't have here an enduring city,*
> *but we seek that which is to come."*
> *Hebrews 13:10-13*

What does "the world" mean"?

Over the centuries the church has oscillated between being either monastically separate from the world, to being one with the world, termed "worldly".

However our Lord Jesus taught us to be neither, but rather, "**IN** the world but not **OF** the world" (John 17:14-16).

In other words, we are to be living physically and present **IN** the world among our community, while at the time living for Christ; being spiritually informed, motivated and empowered by the Holy Spirit as agents **OF** the kingdom of God.

So then, we are not called to leave this **physical world**, or 'Terra firma'. Nor are we called to leave the '**human world**', or our local community in which we live. We are called to live in the world with Christ living through us.

> *"I have been crucified with Christ:*
> *it is no longer I who live, but Christ lives in me:*
> *and the life which I now live in the flesh*
> *I live by the faith in the Son of God,*
> *who loved me and gave Himself for me."*
> *Galatians 2:20*

The Lord Jesus Christ sent us into the world as His witnesses.

> *"But you shall receive power, when the*
> *Holy Spirit has come upon you;*
> *and you shall be witnesses to*
> *Me both in Jerusalem,*
> *and in all Judaea, and Samaria,*
> *and to the end of the earth."*

Acts 1:8

Otherwise, as the apostle Paul observed, we would have to leave this present, physical, literal world to be holy and righteous!

"I wrote unto you in my epistle not to company with sexually immoral people: Yet certainly I did not mean with the sexually immoral people of this world, or with the covetous, or extortioners, or with idolaters;
since then you would need go out of the world."
1Corinthians 5:9-10

We are called by Christ to leave the '**moral world**', or the '*spirit of the world*', known as the *"kosmos"* (G2889), meaning "*the arrangement and order of things*".

"The moral world includes people indifferent or hostile to God, the God-hostile environment generally, and in the widest sense, corruption and evil summed up under the general term "the world."
(journals.sagepub.com)

This 'separation' from the world is not a physical or relational separation. It is a 'spiritual separation' because the disciple of Jesus Christ is operating on diametrically opposed beliefs, values and dynamics to the world.

This is the direct result of the word of God "*sanctifying*" the believer as they obey it. It is the obedience of faith that makes the distinction.

> *"I have given them Your word; and*
> *the world has hated them*
> *because **they are not of the world,***
> ***just as I am not of the world**.*
> *I do not pray that You should take*
> *them out of the world,*
> *but that You should keep them from the evil one.*
> ***They are not of the world, just***
> ***as I am not of the world**.*
> *Sanctify them through Your*
> *truth: Your word is truth.*
> *As You have sent me into the world,*
> ***I also have sent them into the world**."*
> *John 17:14-17*

WE ARE CALLED TO BE IN THE WORLD,
BUT NOT OF THE WORLD

The Church is called out of the world to be in the Body of Christ

In the New Testament the fulfillment of this concept of '*church*' is seen in the formation of the New Testament church. This is where the Lord Jesus Christ called His people "***out of the world***" and to serve Him in and through the church.

> *"And the Lord **added to the church** daily*
> *those who were being saved."*
> *Acts 2:47*
> *"God has **called you together***
> ***in the one body**"*
> *Colossians 3:15 GNTD*

The ultimate fulfillment of the Church will be seen at the 2nd Coming of Christ when the Lord Jesus Christ will miraculously and physically gather all His people, past and present, to "***meet together in the air to ever be with the Lord***". With this in mind God has prepared a house with many mansions for us in heaven (John 14:2).

> *"Then we which are alive and remain*
> *shall be caught up together*
> *with them in the clouds,*

to meet the Lord in the air:
and so shall we ever be with the Lord. "
1Thessalonians 4:17

The 'Universal Church' and the 'Local Church'

The word church is used in the New Testament to refer to either the 'Universal Church' or the 'Local Church'.

The '**Universal Church**' is generally understood to mean **the 'eternal church', to which all born again, children of God belong: past, present and future.**

"For by one Spirit are we all
baptized into one body,
whether we be Jews or Gentiles,
whether we be bond or free;
and have been all made to drink into one Spirit."
1Corinthians 12:13

The '**Local Church**' is the most common usage of the word 'church' in the New Testament and is generally understood to mean **a congregation, or assembly of believers gathered in a given location**.

When the church first started in the New Testament there was only 'one church' in any given location, for example, "the church at Corinth" and the "the church at Rome".

However, with the phenomenal numerical growth of the church and the cultural diversity of Christians throughout the centuries, especially in the modern mega cities, the practical reality of staying as 'one local church' in one city became an impossibility.

Other factors that have contributed to the divesting of the church from 'one church' into 'many churches' in a location has been the emergence of multiple streams and expressions of Christian churches resulting from the various revivals, divisions and differing views on doctrines and practices.

What constitutes a Local Church?

Over the centuries all this change and diversity of expression has impacted on the nature and look of the local church. So how do you recognize a genuine local church from groups and gatherings of Christians?

The simplistic view held by many of what constitutes a

local church finds its basis in the following verse; "*where two or three are gathered in My name, there I am in the midst of them.*" (Matthew 18:20)

However, in this particular verse Jesus is not defining the local church, but rather explaining the power of unity when a quorum of "*two or three*" believers agree together in prayer. The church is more than a 'gathering of Christians', or a prayer meeting. This verse must be interpreted in the context of verses 15-20 in the same chapter.

Another view that has gained a following over the last 25 years or so, even though it is not a new concept, is the 'cell church view', where the 'cell group', or 'house church', is viewed as a church.

However, just as a human single cell does not constitute a human body by itself, as it needs all the other parts joined together to make up the body, so a single cell group of believers by itself does not constitute a local church.

> *"For the body is not one member, but many.*
> *If the foot would say, "Because I'm not*
> *the hand, I'm not part of the body,"*
> *it is not therefore not part of the body.*
> *If the ear would say, "Because I'm not*
> *the eye, I'm not part of the body,"*

it's not therefore not part of the body.
If the whole body were an eye,
where would the hearing be?
If the whole body were hearing,
where would the smelling be?
But now God has set the members,
each one of them,
in the body, just as he desired.
If they were all one member,
where would the body be?
But now they are many members,
but one body."
1Corinthians 12:14-20

The local church is portrayed in the Bible as a '**complete body of believers**'.

Every person, gift and part functioning together as a healthy, growing body. All connected through loving relationships and unified under apostolic vision and leadership. This is the local church!

"Now you are the body of Christ,
and members individually.
God has set some in the church (assembly):
first apostles, second prophets, third teachers,

then miracle workers, then
gifts of healings, helps,
governments, and various kinds of languages."
1Corinthians 12:27-28

"From whom the whole body
fitly joined together
and compacted by that which
every joint supplies,
according to the effectual working
in the measure of every part,
makes increase of the body unto
the edifying of itself in love."
Ephesians 4:16

Jesus' View of the Local Church

Jesus made reference to the Church twice. Once referring to the 'Universal Church' in Matthew 16:15-19 and once referring to the 'Local Church' in Matthew 18:15-20.

From His statements in Matthew 18:15-20 we can see that Jesus Christ described the 'Local Church' as:-

A clearly defined and recognizable group of people..."*tell it to THE CHURCH*"

A group in whom resided the authority of heaven..."*Whatever you bind on EARTH shall be bound in HEAVEN*"

A group of people called to unity in fellowship and prayer..."*If two of you shall AGREE*"

A group of people gathered in the Name of the Lord..."*For where two or three are gathered together in MY NAME*"

The place where Christ promises to be present..."*THERE AM I in the midst*"

The Local Church in the Book of the Acts of the Apostles

The Book of Acts commences with 120 disciples huddled in an upper room for 10 days, waiting for the promised coming of the Holy Spirit.

On the Day of Pentecost when the Holy Spirit came the Church was born as the power of the Holy Spirit ignited these believers to be "*witnesses to Christ*" (Acts 1:8).

The Book of Acts shows us the following 'authorities' that reside in the Local Church:-

The Authority of the Lord Jesus Christ

Luke's opening statement in Acts 1:1 clearly reveals the disciples' understanding that the Lord Jesus Christ was the initiator, owner and builder of the church.

The name of Jesus was the key to the authority of the early church. They acted so boldly and confidently because they remembered the words of the Lord Jesus Christ:-

> *"All authority is given to Me in*
> *heaven and on earth.*
> *Go therefore, and teach all nations,*
> *baptizing them in the name of the*
> *Father, the Son and the Holy Spirit."*
> *Matthew 28:18-19*

The apostles declared the authority of the name of the Lord Jesus Christ as the basis for their preaching and teaching.

> *"Then Peter said unto them, Repent,*
> *and be baptized every one of you in the name*
> *of Jesus Christ for the remission of sins, and*
> *you shall receive the gift of the Holy Spirit."*
> *Acts 2:38*

The authority of the Lord Jesus Christ was central to the ministry and writings of the apostle Paul, who was used by God to write most of the New Testament. It is upon the authority of the Lord Jesus Christ that the church exists and rules in spiritual places.

> *"Which He wrought in Christ, when*
> *He raised Him from the dead,*
> *and set Him at His own right hand*
> *in the heavenly places,*
> *Far above all principality, and power,*
> *and might, and dominion,*
> *and every name that is named, not only in*
> *this world, but also in that which is to come:*
> *And has put all things under His feet,*
> *and gave Him to be the head over*
> *all things to the church,*
> *Which is His body, the fulness*
> *of him that fills all in all."*
> *Ephesians 1:20-23*

The Authority of the Word of God

The New Testament Scriptures, known as the "**apostles' doctrine**" (Acts 2:42), were completed by 90AD at the death of the apostle John. They were accepted as the final authority for life and church practice and have been ever since the beginning of the church.

Over the centuries much care and diligence has been given to the copying, establishing and preservation of the Canon of Scripture, or the 'authoritative Scripture'.

> *"All scripture is given by inspiration of God,*
> *and is profitable for doctrine, for*
> *reproof, for correction,*
> *for instruction in righteousness:*
> *That the man of God may be perfect,*
> *throughly furnished unto all good works."*
> *1Timothy 3:16-17*

The "*apostles' doctrine*" (Acts 2:42), as mentioned before, formed the New Testament Canon, or Scriptures, because the original apostles received these teachings personally and directly from the Lord Jesus Christ Himself.

> *"The former treatise have I made, O Theophilus,*
> *of all that Jesus began both to do and teach,*
> *Until the day in which He was taken up,*
> *after that He through the Holy Spirit*
> *had given commandments unto the*
> *apostles whom He had chosen:*

To whom also He showed Himself alive after
His passion by many infallible proofs,
being seen of them forty days,
and speaking of the things pertaining
to the kingdom of God."
Acts 1:1-3

The church is the "Pillar and Ground of the truth"

"But if I am delayed,
I write so that you may know how you ought
to conduct yourself in the house of God,
which is the church of the living God,
the pillar and ground of the truth."
1Timothy 3:15

The apostle Paul declares here that the church is the "*pillar and ground of the truth*". This is variously translated "the support, bulwark and foundation of the truth" (Amplified Bible and New English Translation), referring to the written Word of God, or the Bible.

He uses the same word, "*pillar*", as Jacob did (Genesis 28:22) to convey the idea that the church, or the house of God, is where the word of God is found, held fast onto and is presented as a light to a lost world.

In his commentary, Ellicott explains that the apostle Paul described the church "*as a massive pillar, upholding and displaying before men and angels the truth - the saving truth of the gospel.*"

> "*...among whom you shine as lights in the world;*
> *Holding fast the word of life...*"
> *Philippians 2:15-16*

The Authority of the Holy Spirit

The early church was founded and established by the Holy Spirit on the Day of Pentecost and beyond. The early church depended on the supernatural presence and power of the Holy Spirit in every aspect of church life.

> "*For it seemed good to us and the Holy Spirit...*"
> *Acts 15:28*

Every local church can only be founded, established and sustained by the supernatural power of the Holy Spirit, otherwise, it is simply a human organization, even though the individual leaders and members may believe in Christ!

The apostle Paul constantly wrote in his epistles about his total dependency upon the Holy Spirit to plant, establish and sustain local churches.

He reminded the Corinthians that their church was planted by him in *"demonstration of the Spirit and power!"*

> *"And my speech and my preaching was not*
> *with enticing words of man's wisdom,*
> *but in **demonstration of the***
> ***Spirit and of power:***
> *That your faith should not stand*
> *in the wisdom of men,*
> *but **in the power of God**."*
> *1 Corinthians 2:4-5*

Later on, some the Corinthians were questioning Paul's authority as an apostle. So he reminded them that the proof of his apostleship was themselves; who were *"written by the Spirit"* and *"ministered through us"*.

> *"Do we begin again to commend ourselves?*
> *or need we, as some others, epistles*
> *of commendation to you,*
> *or letters of commendation from you?*
> *You are our epistle written in our*
> *hearts, known and read of all men:*
> *Forasmuch as ye are manifestly declared*

> *to be the epistle of Christ **ministered
> by us**, written not with ink, **but with
> the Spirit of the living God**;
> not in tables of stone, but in
> fleshy tables of the heart.
> And such trust have we through
> Christ to God-ward:
> Not that we are sufficient of ourselves
> to think any thing as of ourselves;
> but our sufficiency is of God;
> Who also has made us able ministers
> of the new covenant;
> not of the letter, but of the spirit:
> for the letter kills, **but the spirit giveth life**."*
> *2Corinthians 3:1-6*

The Authority of Apostolic Leadership

Throughout the Acts of the Apostles a more structured leadership developed over time, beginning with the appointment of the 12 apostles by Jesus Christ to lead the church in Jerusalem.

This was necessary as the church in Jerusalem grew and many other leaders emerged in the church. Examples of these new leaders were the '7 deacons' (Acts 6), Philip, the evangelist (Acts 8) and Barnabas and Saul, the apostles in Antioch (Acts 9 &13).

The responsibility of the oversight, pastoring and direction of the local church rested with these leaders, who were initially called "Elders" after the Jewish tradition and in recent history "Ministers" and "Pastors".

*"The **elders** who are among you I exhort,*
*I who am a **fellow elder**, and a witness*
of the sufferings of Christ,
and also a partaker of the glory
that will be revealed:
***Shepherd (pastor)** the flock of*
God which is among you,
***serving as overseers**,*
not by compulsion, but willingly; not
for dishonest gain, but eagerly;
nor as being lords over those entrusted to
you, but being examples to the flock."
1Peter 5:1-3

Later, especially with the emergence of Paul and others, the term "elder" was broadened to incorporate the concept of '*giftedness*', as listed in Ephesians 4:11, not just position, sex or age.

*"And he gave **some, apostles;**
and some, prophets;
and some, evangelists; and some,
pastors and teachers;
For the perfecting of the saints,
for the work of the ministry,
for the edifying of the body of Christ"*
Ephesians 4:11-12

The apostle Paul articulated the concept that 'giftedness' produced levels of leadership in the church. In other words, there was an 'order of authority' in the church, which he outlined to the Corinthians:-

*"And God has appointed these in the church,
first apostles, secondarily
prophets, thirdly teachers,
after that miracles, **then** gifts of healings, helps,
governments, diversities of tongues."*
1Corinthians 12:28

For example, the local church in Jerusalem was led by the 12 apostles with the seniority of James, Peter and John.

"And when James, Cephas (Peter) and

> *John, who seemed to be pillars,*
> *perceived the grace that was given unto me,*
> *they gave to me and Barnabas the*
> *right hand of fellowship."*
> *Gal 2:9*

Also, the local church in Antioch was led by a team of "*prophets and teachers*" with the seniority of Barnabas.

> *"Now there were in the church that was at*
> *Antioch certain prophets and teachers;*
> *as Barnabas, and Simeon who was*
> *called Niger, and Lucius of Cyrene, and*
> *Manaen, who had been brought up*
> *with Herod the tetrarch, and Saul."*
> *Acts 13:1*

The 'Fellowship of Apostles'

We observe that even though the great apostle Paul knew his own apostolic authority in Christ, he still sought out the recognition and confirmation by the other established apostles, as he declared, "*lest by any means I should run, or had run, in vain.*"

> *"And I went up by revelation,*

and communicated unto them that gospel
which I preach among the Gentiles,
but privately to **them which**
were of reputation,
lest by any means I should
run, or had run, in vain.
And when James, Cephas, and John,
who seemed to be pillars,
perceived the grace that was given unto me,
they gave to me and Barnabas
the right hand of fellowship;
that we should go to the heathen,
and they to the circumcision."
Galatians 2:2,9

Just as we understand that believers ought to be under the authority of leaders and leaders ought to submit to apostles, we see here modeled the need for the apostolic leaders to be mutually submitting to other apostolic leaders in a 'fellowship of apostles'.

We can observe this occurring more and more in the present day with apostolic leaders connecting, fellowshipping and cooperating nationally and globally for the cause of the Gospel. One such example is the *'Empowered21'* movement, which coordinates the connection and cooperation of major Pentecostal leaders across the world.

The Authority of Locality

This principle of the authority of the local church is clearly seen in practice when members of the Jerusalem local church were acting improperly in the Antioch local church. A whole chapter is devoted to this controversy.

Paul and Barnabas and other representatives of the Antioch local church came to Jerusalem to discuss the matter with the local church leaders in Jerusalem.

Here we see the principle of the recognition of the authority of the local church. The apostles of the Jerusalem church did not have authority over or in the local church in Antioch.

> *"And certain men came down from*
> *Judaea taught the brethren, and said,*
> *Except you are circumcised after the*
> *manner of Moses, you cannot be saved.*
> *When therefore Paul and Barnabas had*
> *no small dissension and disputation with*
> *them, they determined that Paul and*
> *Barnabas, and certain others of them,*

> *should go up to Jerusalem to the apostles
> and elders about this question."*
> *Acts 15:1-2*

Most of the Epistles in the New Testament were written to Local Churches

Most of the New Testament was written to local churches. For example, "*the church at Corinth*" (1Corinthians 1:1-2), "*the church at Ephesus*" (Ephesians 1:1), "*the church at Philippi*" (Philippians 1:1) and "*the church at Thessaloniki*" (1Thessalonians 1:1). The epistle to the Galatians was written to all the local "*Churches of the Galatia*" (Galatians 1:1-2).

The following statement is very helpful in defining and summarizing what constitutes a local church:-

**"A LOCAL CHURCH IS
SELF GOVERNING,
SELF SUPPORTING
AND
SELF PROPAGATING"**

We will deal with each of these characteristics of what constitutes a local church in detail in chapter five.

Chapter Five

THE LOCAL CHURCH IS SELF GOVERNING, SELF SUPPORTING AND SELF PROPAGATING

We will deal with each of these characteristics in detail.

THE LOCAL CHURCH IS ' SELF GOVERNING'

The Local Church has authority in itself because of the nature in which it was planted, established and developed through the operation of spiritual authority, or 'apostolic authority'.

> *"And I say also unto you, That you are Peter,*
> *and upon this rock I will build my church;*
> *and the gates of hell shall not prevail against it.*
> *And I will give unto you the keys*
> *of the kingdom of heaven:*

and whatever you shall bind on earth
shall be bound in heaven:
and whatever you shall loose on earth
shall be loosed in heaven."
Matthew 16:18-19

A local church comes into being as a result
of being birthed, planted and established
through an 'apostolic person', commonly
called a 'founding leader' or 'church planter'.
*"**I planted**, Apollos watered;*
but God gave the increase.
So then neither he who plants is
anything, nor he who waters,
but God who gives the increase."
1Corinthians 3:6-7

An apostolic person is also called a 'visionary leader' by virtue of a divine vision and calling to plant a particular local church.

Another term for an apostolic person is a 'spiritual father or mother' because of the particular way in which a local church is formed. A local church is 'birthed in the spirit', not established by natural means or method.

"For though you have ten thousand
instructors in Christ,
yet you don't have not many fathers:
for in Christ Jesus I have begotten
you through the gospel."
1Corinthians 4:15

We see this same pattern of the importance of apostolic authority in the planting of the church in Antioch. The original apostles of the local church in Jerusalem authorized and sent Barnabas as an apostle, or 'a sent one', to plant a church in the city of Antioch where many people were turning to Christ.

"But some of them were men
of Cyprus and Cyrene,
who, when they had come to Antioch,
spoke to the Hellenists,
preaching the Lord Jesus.
And the hand of the Lord was with them:
and a great number believed,
and turned unto the Lord.
Then news of these things came to the
ears of the church in Jerusalem:
and they sent out Barnabas,

to go as far as Antioch.
When he came and had seen the grace of
God, he was glad, and encouraged them all
that with purpose of heart they
would continue with the Lord.
For he was a good man, full of
the Holy Spirit and of faith.
And a great many people was
added unto the Lord."
Acts 11:20-24

After a few years, the apostolic team in the local church in Antioch separated and sent Barnabas and Saul to go as apostles to plant churches.

"First apostles"

"And God has set some in the
*church, **first apostles,***
secondarily prophets, thirdly teachers,
after that miracles, then gifts of healings, helps,
governments, diversities of tongues."
1Corinthians 12:28

The traditional usage of the Greek word "*apostolos*" (G652), apostle in English, was used to describe "a delegate, messenger, ambassador, or one sent forth with orders" (Strongs Concordance).

The Oxford Dictionary gives a fuller and broader meaning to apostles:-

> *"A pioneering missionary, a vigorous*
> *and pioneering advocate*
> *or supporter of a concept, particular*
> *policy, idea or cause."*

In the New Testament an apostle came to be understood as a person called and sent by God to preach the Gospel and plant churches. The role of the apostle was foundational in pioneering and establishing local churches and ensuring their ongoing viability and health. Therefore, the apostle Paul placed apostles as "*first*" in the order of things.

> *"According to the grace of God which is*
> *given unto me, as a **wise master-builder**,*
> *I have **laid the foundation**, and*
> *another builds thereon.*
> *But let every man take heed how he builds upon.*
> *For other foundation can no man lay than*

that is laid, which is Jesus Christ."
1Corinthians 3:10-11

The Vision of the Local Church is in the heart of an Apostle

The Pioneering Spirit of the Apostle

The apostle Paul's use of the words *"first apostles"* (1Corinthians 12:28) is important, as the word *"first"* is *"proton"* (G4412) in the original Greek language, meaning "first in time or place, rank, influence, honor". A related word is *"prototypos"* (Wiktionary), or 'prototype', meaning, "an original form, impression, mould or pattern".

The core idea, therefore, is that the apostle as *"a wise master builder"* is to be the pattern, blueprint, mould, and pioneer upon which the local church is birthed, planted, constructed and sustained.

Consequently, the other leaders such as prophets, evangelists, pastors and teachers are to build upon the apostolic foundation and according to the apostolic pattern, or blue print.

"For *we* are *laborers together* with God*:*
you are God *'s* husbandry, *you*
are God *'s* building.
According *to* the grace *of* God *which is*
given *unto* me, ***as a wise masterbuilder***,
I have laid *the* foundation, and
another builds thereon.
But *let every* man *take* heed
how *he builds on it.*"
1Corinthians 3:9-10

The signs of an apostle

There are several signs given by the apostle Paul of his apostolic ministry. These are helpful in identifying what constitutes a local church, or an 'apostolic church'.

The first two signs are apostolic "**patience**", or longevity, which is accompanied with "**signs and wonders and mighty deeds**", or the supernatural.

"Truly the signs of an apostle were
accomplished among you
in all patience, in signs, and
wonders, and mighty deeds."
2Corinthians 12:12

The local church by it's very spiritual nature is birthed and established supernaturally.

Every local church is to be the "*gate of heaven*" (Genesis 28:17), exercising spiritual authority and power to their community where the miracle of transformed lives through the new birth is the centerpiece.

The third sign of an apostle is the '**fruit of souls**". The apostle Paul placed the miracle of 'soul winning' and birthing non believers into Christ high among his credentials as an apostle.

> "***You are our epistle written in our hearts***, *known and read by all men:*
> ***Clearly you are an epistle of Christ ministered by us***,
> *written not with ink, but by the Spirit of the living God;*
> *not in tablets of stone, but on tablets of flesh, that is, of the heart."*
> *2Corinthians 3:2-3*

> *"Am I not an apostle? am I not free?*
> *have I not seen Jesus Christ our Lord?*
> ***are you not my work in the Lord?***

> *If I am not an apostle to others,*
> *yet doubtless I am to you:*
> ***for you are the seal of my***
> ***apostleship in the Lord.***"
> *1Corinthians 9:2*

In the current urban and 'Christianized' West, however, the apostolic sign of the fruit of souls can easily be lost because of the large numbers of professing Christians already existing in many communities.

As a result, churches can more easily be 'started' on the basis of attracting existing Christians rather than pioneering and planting supernaturally through 'soul winning' and disciple making among the unchurched in the community.

The fourth sign of an apostle is the **confirmation and witness of established apostles**.

The apostle Paul was originally sought out and established into leadership by Barnabas, the senior leader, or 'apostle', in the local church at Antioch.

Then, 14 years later Barnabas and Saul received confirmation of their apostleship from the existing apostles in Jerusalem, especially from Peter, James and John, the "*pillars*" or senior apostles.

> *"Then departed Barnabas to*
> *Tarsus, for to seek Saul:*
> *And when he had found him, he*
> *brought him unto Antioch.*
> *And it came to pass, that a whole year they*
> *assembled themselves with the church,*
> *and taught much people. And the disciples*
> *were called Christians first in Antioch."*
> *Acts11:25-26*

> *"Then fourteen years after I went up*
> *again to Jerusalem with Barnabas,*
> *and took Titus with me also.*
> *And I went up by revelation, and*
> *communicated unto them*
> *that gospel which I preach among the Gentiles,*
> *but privately to them which were of reputation,*
> *lest by any means I should run,*
> *or had run, in vain."*
> *Galatians 2:1-3*

The Lord Jesus Christ modeled this approach when He asked to be baptized by John the Baptist, even though

He knew that His calling and ministry would be greater and more effective than John.

*"Then Jesus came from Galilee to the
Jordan to John, to be baptized by him.
But John would have hindered him, saying,
"I need to be baptized by you,
and you come to me?"
But Jesus, answering, said to him, "Allow it now,
for this is the fitting way for us to
fulfill all righteousness."
Then he allowed him."
Matthew 3:13-15*

It is important to notice in all these examples that bonafide apostles always seek out and establish relationships with other apostles.

The apostle Paul termed this "*the right hand of fellowship*", when the apostles of the local church in Jerusalem met with the apostles of the local church of Antioch to discuss and recognize spheres of apostolic authority and ministry. Here we observe the recognition of another level of apostolic leadership which reached out to whole ethnic groups rather than just a locality.

"...for He who appointed Peter to the **apostleship of the circumcision** *(Jews)*
appointed me also to the Gentiles;
and when they perceived the
grace that was given to me,
James and Cephas and John, they
who were reputed to be pillars,
gave to me and Barnabas the
right hand of fellowship,
that we should go to the Gentiles,
and they to the circumcision."
Galatians 2:8-9

The heart of an apostle - "care" and "deep concern"

When murmurs and questions arose in the Corinthian church about Paul's ministry and authority, he lists the pain and sufferings he had endured as an apostle:-

"...in labor's...stripes...prisons...
beaten...stoned...shipwrecked...
journeys...perils weariness and
toil...sleeplessness...
hunger and thirst...fasting...
cold and nakedness..."
2Corinthians 11:21-28

At the end of the list he exclaims that "**beside the other things**", it was his daily, internal care and a "**deep concern for all the churches**" that burdened him the most!

> *"Beside the other things, what*
> *comes upon me daily,*
> ***my deep concern (care)*** *of all the churches."*
> *2Corinthians 11:28*

This is the heart of a true apostle. Not a job, not a ministry, not a position, not even success (which Paul certainly had) and not even sufferings and trials. The apostle carries God's people in their heart with a divine jealousy for Christ!

> *"For I am jealous for you with godly jealousy:*
> *for I have betrothed you to one husband,*
> *that I may present you as a*
> *chaste virgin to Christ."*
> *2Corinthians 11:2*

The fifth sign of an apostle is the possession of faith and the ability to be **financially self funding.**

The apostle Paul, for example, was 'bi-vocational' to support his team and apostolic ministry. He worked regularly at his trade as a tent maker, alongside raising finances from offerings from the local churches that he had planted

> *"So because he was of the same trade,*
> **he stayed with them and worked**;
> *for by occupation they were* **tentmakers**.
> *And he reasoned in the*
> *synagogue every sabbath,*
> *and persuaded the Jews and the Greeks."*
> *Acts 18:3-4*
> **"And labour, working with our own hands**:
> *being reviled, we bless; being*
> *persecuted, we suffer it:"*
> *1Corinthians 4:12*

The role of movements and denominations

Over the centuries this 'relational connection' among apostles and local churches shifted and became more and more structured, eventually removing the authority from the local churches and the apostles to a more centralized, hierarchical and denominational authority.

The Reformation which started in around 1517 by Luther and others reacted to this centralization and developed the concept of local congregations ruled by elders, called **'congregationalism'**.

This change would begin to restore authority back to the local church.

A recent trend, especially with the advent of the Pentecostal revival in the early 1900s, has been the emergence of 'movements of churches'. Generally, these relationally based movements, as opposed to the centralized and structural denominations, recognize the importance of the autonomy of the local church.

These kinds of '**movements of local churches**' tend to operate within more organic, cooperative and flexible structures that provide:-

- relationships and connection for pastors and leaders

- a set of agreed policies for integrity, accountability and wellbeing

- coordinating resources that empower the local church leaders in their particular vision and ministry rather than operating a central control and vision from the denominational headquarters

- assistance with advice and support with problems and challenges

As a result, local churches that operate connected to a 'relational movement' tend to experience significantly higher rates of health, growth and expansion than their denominational counterparts.

For example, research organizations like the NCLS (National Church Life Survey) in Australia, has discovered that burnout rates among 'denominational' pastors and leaders are significantly higher than amongst those in 'relational, local church movements' pastors and leaders ("Burnout in Church Leaders", Kaldor and Bullpit).

THE LOCAL CHURCH IS 'SELF-SUPPORTING'

The House of God has always been ordained by God to be His "**Storehouse**" for His people; a place of blessing, favor, provision, prosperity and supply.

> *"Bring all the tithes into the **storehouse**,*
> *that there may be food in **My house**,*
> *and prove me now herewith,*
> *says the Lord of Hosts,*
> *if I will not **open to you the windows of**
> ***heaven,** and pour you out a blessing,*

> *that there shall not be room*
> *enough to receive it."*
> *Malachi 3:10*

The very first example of the House of God is revealed in the Garden of Eden. Here God placed Adam and Eve into a haven and place of fellowship with Him.

It was from the Garden, or the 'House of God', that Adam and Eve were to rule and preside over God's creation as stewards and beneficiaries of His love, blessings and favor.

The first mention of the House of God is found in Genesis 28 where Jacob received his revelation from God in the place he called "*Bethel", or "the "House of God*".

As a direct result of receiving this dream Jacob committed himself to building God's House on this place and supporting God's House through giving "*the tithe*"; a tenth of his income.

Jacob was repeating what all God's people had done in the past and would do in the future; willingly supporting God's House through tithes and offerings so it would be self funding.

*"And he called the name of that
place **Bethel (House of God)**
but the name of that city was
called Luz at the first.
And Jacob vowed a vow, saying,
If God will be with me,
and will keep me in this way that I go,
and will give me bread to eat,
and raiment to put on,
So that I come again to my
father's house in peace;
then shall the Lord be my God:
And this stone, which I have set for
a pillar, shall be **God's house:**
and of all that you shall give me **I will
surely give the tenth unto You**."
Genesis 28:19-22*

Another great example of supply in the House of God is seen in the wilderness journey by the children of Israel. Two things emerge from this experience.

First, God called His people "**the church in the wilderness**" (Acts 7:38).

Second, they were to fund the construction and ongoing

maintenance and ministry of the Tabernacle, the "*House of God*", through the giving of "*Tithes and Offerings*".

> "*Thus you also shall* **offer a heave offering**
> **unto the Lord of all your tithes***,*
> *which you receive of the children of Israel;*
> *and you shall give thereof the Lord's*
> *heave offering to Aaron the priest.*"
> *Leviticus 18:28*

The local church is the House of God in this present age

> "*But if I tarry long,*
> *that you might know how you ought to*
> *behave yourself in the* **House of God***,*
> **which is the Church of the living God***,*
> *the pillar and ground of the truth.*"
> *1Timothy 3:15*

This 'Church age' commenced with this declaration of Jesus Christ:-

> "*And I say also unto you, That you are Peter,*
> *and upon this rock* **I will build my church***;*

and the gates of hell shall not prevail against it."
Matthew 16:18

This will climax with the glorification of the church at the 2nd coming of Christ.

"That He might present it (the church)
*to Himself **a glorious church**,*
not having spot, or wrinkle, or any such thing;
but that it should be holy and without blemish."
Ephesians 5:27

As it has been from the beginning, God's people are to voluntarily fund God's House and its ongoing 'vision and ministry' through the giving of Tithes and Offerings.

The apostle Paul explains this to the church at Corinth when he likens the financial support of the leaders of the church to the priests in the Old Testament temple.

"Do you not know that they who
minister about holy things
live of the things of the temple
(the "Tithes and Offerings")?
*and they who wait at the altar are **partakers***

with the altar *(Tithes and Offerings)?*
Even so the Lord has ordained that
they who preach the gospel
*should **live of the gospel***
(Tithes and Offerings)."
1Corinthians 9:13-14

The writer to the Hebrews says exactly the same thing. He declared that Christ's ministry as our *"High Priest after the Order of Melchizedek"* received Tithes before the law from Abraham and continues to receive Tithes after the law in the church age, because His priesthood is eternal.

"And truly they that are of the sons of Levi,
who receive the office of the priesthood,
have a commandment to take tithes of
the people according to the law,
that is, of their brethren, though they
come out of the loins of Abraham:
But He (Melchizedek) whose descent
is not counted from them
received tithes of Abraham, and
blessed him that had the promises.
And without all contradiction the
less is blessed of the better.

And here men that die receive tithes; but
there He (Melchizedek) receives them,
of whom it is witnessed that He lives.
Hebrews 7:5-8

"(For those priests were made without an oath;
but this with an oath by Him that said unto him,
The Lord swore and will not repent,
You are a priest for ever after the
order of Melchizedek:)
By so much was Jesus made a
surety of a better testament."
Hebrews 7:21-22

Where should I bring my Tithes and Offerings?

Many Christians have asked this question: "where do I bring my tithes and offerings?"

When we understand the centrality of the local church in God's work on the earth, the answer is obvious: "to my local church family". We are to bring our tithes and offerings to the place where we are planted, established, nourished and mobilized as a minister into the marketplace.

Every local church is to be self funding in order to fulfil it's divine purpose and ministry to their local community and beyond. This becomes even more important as a local church begins to grow, develop and emerge as an 'apostolic community of faith'.

Where do Boards and Leadership Teams fit in?

As a local church grows and develops 'apostolic authority' beyond it's immediate locality, it will by nature be receiving larger amounts of finance. This is a direct result of the health, commitment and influence of the local church family.

This is where proven and trustworthy teams need to be formed at various levels within the local church such as Boards, Trustees and Executive Teams to oversee and steward the funds that are given by the members of the church.

Furthermore, there should diligent and professional accounting of the funds received and expended, and open transparency back to members of the local church. This is best achieved through independent, annual audits and Annual General Meetings of the members.

Leadership is always outworked through teams

Even though leadership is a gift, anointing and calling on an individual, leadership in the New Testament was never exercised individually or in a vacuum. True Apostolic leadership is always outworked through teams - together!

This is why bonafide apostolic leaders know the importance of forming teams around them, which provides accountability and transparency to the local church membership and beyond.

THE LOCAL CHURCH IS 'SELF PROPAGATING'

When a local church becomes 'self governing' through it's apostolic leadership and 'self funding' through receiving tithes and offerings it will be positioned to effectively fulfill the mission of Christ by becoming 'self propagating', or to reproduce itself.

This mission is the evangelization of the world and the building of the church of Christ through church planting. This is the power of self propagation at work!

> *"But you shall receive power when
> the Holy Spirit comes on you,*

and you shall be witnesses unto me,
both in Jerusalem, Judea, Samaria
and to the ends of the earth."
Acts 1:8

"...and the Lord added to the church
daily those who were being saved."
Acts 2:47

Many denominational structures and especially the recent emphasis on the 'campus', or 'multi-site model' can tend to centralize and structure authority around one charismatic, senior leader.

However, this approach can limit the reproduction and multiplication of apostolic leadership. As a result, the propagation of the local church through church planting can be diminished because potential and rising leaders can only stay within the one centralized authority structure of the 'home church'.

The campus model has proven to be an effective outreach tool within large metropolitan centers. However, the body of Christ also needs a multiplication in the number of foundational, apostolic leaders to pioneer and plant new churches outside the 'home church' to "*where Christ is not named*".

> *"And so I have made it my aim*
> *to preach the gospel,*
> *not where Christ was named, lest I should*
> *build upon another man's foundation:*
> *But as it is written, To whom he was*
> *not spoken of, they shall see:*
> *and they that have not heard shall understand."*
> *Romans 15:20-21*

Every local church, therefore, is ordained by God to be a 'leadership incubator', reproducing all the leadership gifts of apostles, prophets, evangelists, pastors and teachers.

The Antioch example

A good example of the raising up and releasing of apostolic leadership is found in the local church at Antioch. In Acts 13 we see the local church's original leadership team of "*prophets and teachers*" ministering and leading with Barnabas, an apostle, who was sent from Jerusalem to plant the church.

As a result Saul rises to be an apostle beside Barnabas and together they are recognized, released and sent by the local church leadership team to plant churches. The leadership team continued to lead the local church at Antioch.

> *"Now there were in the church that was at*
> *Antioch certain prophets and teachers;*
> *as Barnabas, and Simeon that was*
> *called Niger, and Lucius of Cyrene,*
> *and Manaen, who had been brought up*
> *with Herod the tetrarch, and Saul.*
> *As they ministered to the Lord, and*
> *fasted, the Holy Spirit said,*
> *Separate me Barnabas and Saul for the*
> *work to which I have called them.*
> *And when they had fasted and prayed,*
> *and laid their hands on them,*
> *they sent them away.*
> *So they, being sent by the Holy Spirit ,*
> *departed unto Seleucia; and from*
> *there they sailed to Cyprus."*
> *Acts 13:1-4*

Finding the balance

Finding the balance is important. That is, how to grow

and expand the local church within it's community and beyond by using methods like the campus, or multi-site model, while at the same time growing and expanding the kingdom of God through pioneering and church planting into other communities, regions, ethnicities and nations.

The only way that this can effectively occur is through the raising up of apostolic leaders within the local church, who are then released to go and plant new local churches beyond the sending church.

The Church GATHERED and the Church SCATTERED

*"Therefore they that were **scattered abroad**
went every where preaching the word.
Then Philip went down to the city of
Samaria, and preached Christ unto them.
And the people with one accord gave heed
unto those things which Philip spake, hearing
and seeing the miracles which he did."*
Acts 8:4-6

We have previously discussed the importance of the church '**gathered**', or assembled and congregated.

However, an equally important concept of the church is that it should also be '**scattered**', or dispersed, into the world to be witnesses within their particular communities.

We see this in the teaching of Jesus Christ, when He presented the two characteristics of His disciples; "**LIGHT**" and "**SALT**".

*"You are the **salt of the earth**…*
*You are the **light of the world.***
A city that is set on a hill cannot be hid."
Matthew 5:13-14

"**Light**" as a visible *"city on a hill"* is a picture of the church **GATHERED** together, whereas, "**salt**" is a picture of the church **SCATTERED** into the world to bring the flavor, taste and the experience of Christ to a lost humanity.

The propagation of the local church
occurs at the point of scattering

The New Testament Examples of Church Planting

There are five New Testament examples of church planting presented by Luke in the Acts of the Apostles that have common features.

1. The 1st Church in Jerusalem

*"But Peter, standing up with the eleven,
lifted up his voice, and said unto them,
You men of Judaea, and all you
that dwell at Jerusalem,
be this known unto you, and
hearken to my words...
Now when they heard this, they
were pricked in their heart,
and said unto Peter and to the
rest of the apostles,
Men and brethren, what shall we do?
Then Peter said unto them, Repent,
and be baptized every one of you
in the name of Jesus Christ for
the remission of sins,
and you shall receive the gift of the Holy Spirit.
And with many other words did he
testify and exhort, saying,
Save yourselves from this untoward generation.*

Then they that gladly received
his word were baptized:
and the same day there were added unto
them about three thousand souls.
And they continued steadfastly in the
apostles' doctrine and fellowship,
and in breaking of bread, and in prayers.
And the Lord added to the church
daily such as should be saved."
Acts 2:41-42, 47

2. **The Church in Samaria**

"Therefore they that were scattered abroad
went every where preaching the word.
Then Philip went down to the city of Samaria,
and preached Christ unto them.
And the people with one accord gave heed
unto those things which Philip spake,
hearing and seeing the miracles which he did.
For unclean spirits, crying with loud voice,
came out of many that were
possessed with them:
and many taken with palsies, and
that were lame, were healed.

And there was great joy in that city...
Now when the apostles which
were at Jerusalem heard
that Samaria had received the word of God,
they sent Peter and John to them*:*
Who, when they were come
down, prayed for them,
that they might receive the Holy Spirit:
(For as yet He was fallen upon none of them:
only they were baptized in the
name of the Lord Jesus.)
Then laid they their hands on them,
and they received the Holy Spirit...
And they, when they had testified and
preached the word of the Lord,
returned to Jerusalem, and preached the gospel
in many villages of the Samaritans..."
Acts 8:5-8, 14-17, 25

3. The Church in Antioch

"Now they which were scattered abroad
upon the persecution that arose about Stephen
travelled as far as Phenice, and
Cyprus, and Antioch,

preaching the word to none
but unto the Jews only.
And some of them were men
of Cyprus and Cyrene,
who, when they were come to Antioch,
spake unto the Grecians,
preaching the Lord Jesus.
And the hand of the Lord was with them:
and a great number believed,
and turned unto the Lord.
Then tidings of these things came unto
the ears of the church which was in
*Jerusalem: and **they sent Barnabas**,*
that he should go as far as Antioch.
Who, when he came, and had seen the grace
of God, was glad, and exhorted them all,
that with purpose of heart they
would cleave unto the Lord.
For he was a good man, and full of
the Holy Spirit and of faith:
and many people was added unto the Lord.
Then departed Barnabas to
Tarsus, for to seek Saul:
And when he had found him, he
brought him unto Antioch.
And it came to pass, that a whole year

**they assembled themselves with the
church**, *and taught many people.
And* **the disciples were called
Christians first in Antioch.** *"*
Acts 11:19-26

4. The Church in Corinth

*"After these things Paul departed from
Athens, and came to Corinth;
And he found a certain Jew named
Aquila, born in Pontus,
who had recently come from
Italy with his wife Priscilla
(because Claudius had commanded
all Jews to depart from Rome);
and came to them.
So, because he was of the same trade,
he stayed with them and worked:
for by occupation they were tentmakers...
And he departed from there and entered
the house of a certain man named Justus,
one who worshipped God, whose house
was next door to the synagogue.
Then Crispus, the ruler of the synagogue,
believed on the Lord with all his household.
And many of the Corinthians, hearing,
believed and were baptized."
Acts 18:1-3, 7-8*

5. The Church in Ephesus

*"Now a certain Jew named
Apollos, born at Alexandria,
an eloquent man, and mighty in the
Scriptures, came to Ephesus.
This man had been instructed in the way of
the Lord; and being fervent in the spirit,
he spoke and taught accurately
the things of the Lord,
though he knew only the baptism of John.
So he began to speak boldly in the synagogue.
When Aquila and Priscilla heard
him, they took him aside
and explained to him the way
of God more accurately.
And when he desired to cross to Achaia,
the brethren wrote, exhorting the
disciples to receive him;
and when he arrived, he greatly helped
those who had believed through grace:
For he vigorously refuted the Jews publicly,
showing from the scriptures
that Jesus is the Christ...
And it happened, while Apollos was at Corinth,
that Paul, having passed through the*

*upper regions came to Ephesus
and finding some disciples, He said to them,
Have you received the Holy
Spirit when you believed?
So they said to him,
We have not so much as heard
whether there is a Holy Spirit.
And he said to them, Into what
then were you baptized?
And they said, Into John's baptism.
Then said Paul, John indeed baptized
with a baptism of repentance,
saying to the people, that they
should believe on Him
who would come after him,
that is, on Christ Jesus.
When they heard this, they were baptized
in the name of the Lord Jesus.
And when Paul had laid hands on them,
the Holy Spirit came upon them; and they
spoke with tongues, and prophesied.
Now the men were about twelve in all...
And this continued for two years,
so that all who dwelt in Asia heard
the word of the Lord Jesus,
both Jews and Greeks.*

Now God worked unusual miracles
by the hands of Paul,
so that even handkerchiefs or aprons were
brought from his body to the sick,
and the diseases left them and the
evil spirits went out of them."
Acts 18:24-28; 19:1-7,10-12

From these accounts we can observe that the first local church, in Jerusalem, was birthed sovereignly and supernaturally on the Day of Pentecost. This occurred when the Holy Spirit fell upon the apostles and disciples.

On that day the 1st New Testament local church was instantly established, which grew very quickly to an estimated 15-20 thousand new members.

New Testament local church common features

Although the other four examples in the book of Acts of the Apostles were not so dramatic in terms of time frame, they all show the same common features as the church in Jerusalem such as:-

- The planting of a new local church by an apostolic person

- The evangelism of the unchurched

- The preaching of the Gospel calling people to repentance and faith in Jesus Christ

- The supernatural demonstration of the Gospel with healings, signs and wonders

- The initiation and confirmation of new believers through water baptism

- The prayer for receiving the baptism in the Holy Spirit for all believers

- The discipling of the new believers in the teachings and commands of Jesus Christ

- The confirmation of the new local church by recognized apostles

- The recognition of local leaders as the spiritual authority of the local church

- The financial, self funding of the local church through tithes and offerings

- The propagation of the local church to other cities

- The recognition of apostles and other ministries by the local church

The chain reaction of Self Propagation

When local churches are effectively self propagating a chain reaction is ignited. The results are increased levels of evangelism, discipleship, leadership development, quality and quantity growth and the increase of planting new churches.

The cycle of Self Propagation

The ongoing cycle of self propagation can be observed commencing with the sending of Barnabas from Jerusalem, his home church, to Antioch. This resulted in the raising of the great apostle Paul, the gospel being preached and churches planted throughout the world. Most of the New Testament was written at this time!

Phase #1 - The Church in Jerusalem

In the church in Jerusalem we observe the cycle of self propagation in operation from Acts 1 through to Acts 9; win lost people, make disciples, raise leaders, release apostles by the sending of Barnabas to plant the church in Antioch.

Phase #2 - The Church in Antioch

When Barnabas arrives in Antioch we observe the same cycle from Acts 9 through to Acts 13; win lost people, make disciples, raise leaders, release apostles by the sending of Barnabas and Paul to plant churches.

Phase #3 - The New Testament Churches

As soon as Barnabas and Paul were sent from Antioch the same cycle began again; win lost people, make disciples, raise leaders, send apostles by being the sending of Timothy to Ephesus and Titus to Crete. Other apostles and ministers such as Epahroditus, Apollos, Aquila and Priscilla, Artemas, Tychicus, Junia and many others continued the work of church church planting with Paul.

Chapter Six

THE HOUSE OF PRAYER

Prayer was central to the spiritual life and vitality of the first church in Jerusalem. Prayer was not only an individual practice, it was also a corporate one.

> *"And they continued steadfastly in the apostles' doctrine and fellowship, and in breaking of bread, and in prayers."*
> *Acts 2:42*

The church was founded in a prayer meeting as the disciples waited at the command of Christ for ten days prior to the Day of Pentecost. Then, suddenly, the Holy Spirit descended in power and the first church was inaugurated!

> *"These all continued with one accord*

> *in prayer and supplication,*
> *with the women, and Mary the mother*
> *of Jesus, and with his brethren.*
> *Acts 1:14*

The leaders of the churches in Jerusalem and Antioch knew the value of praying together to seek the mind and guidance of the Lord.

> *"But we will give ourselves continually to*
> *prayer, and to the ministry of the word."*
> *Acts 6:4*

> *"As they ministered to the Lord, and*
> *fasted, the Holy Spirit said,*
> *Separate me Barnabas and Saul for the*
> *work whereunto I have called them.*
> *And when they had fasted and prayed,*
> *and laid their hands on them,*
> *they sent them away."*
> *Acts 13:2-3*

This habit of corporate prayer continued all through the Acts of the Apostles because prayer was the hallmark of the New Testament church.

"And said unto them, It is written,
My house shall be called the house of prayer;
but you have made it a den of thieves."
Matthew 21:13

The church that prays together stays together!

Prayer is not just about finding out what God wants to do through the church, it is more about what God wants to do in the church! Prayer leads us into a deeper trust and dependency upon God and develops unity among the members of the church.

"Confess your faults to one another,
and pray one for another, that
you may be healed.
The effectual fervent prayer of a
righteous man avails much."
James 5:16

Unity of heart and mind flows from praying together. There is something very special and powerful about regular, consistent corporate prayer in the local church. It becomes the oil that keeps everyone and everything running smoothly.

Prayer should not just be a call to pray together because

there is a problem or crisis. Prayer baths the whole local church in the presence of the Holy Spirit. So when problems arise, and they will, the church will be on the front foot, ready, unified and powerful! Prayerfulness causes us to be filled with prayer.

> *"Continue in prayer, and watch in*
> *the same with thanksgiving."*
> *Colossians 4:2*

The importance of prayer targets

In our church in Brisbane, we have found over many years that having prayer targets that the whole church was praying for kept prayer alive and active and built an incredible sense of unity. This is because all the members were moving in the same direction.

One of the most important targets was prayer for the unchurched to discover salvation in Christ. We made this specific by asking every member to compile a prayer list of unsaved friends, family and associates and the whole church prayed and agreed in faith for supernatural outcomes.

Pray "*first of all*"

The apostle Paul encouraged that prayer is a "**first of all**" priority for the believer…not a last resort!

> "*I exhort therefore, that, **first of all**, supplications, prayers, intercessions, and giving of thanks, be made for all men.*"

Prayer is so important because, "*first of all*", prayer is our time in connection and relationship with God.

Second, Prayer is the creative, power of faith language into our lives, world and circumstances. Prayer is not about earth speaking to heaven it is about heaven speaking to earth through the agreement of faith and bringing about heaven's viewpoint and answers into the earth.

> "*Again I say unto you, That if two of you shall agree on earth as touching any thing that they shall ask, it shall be done for them by my Father who is in heaven.*"
> *Matthew 18:19*

Third, Prayer is working with and agreeing with God. Prayer is God's method.

> *"If my people, who are called by my name,*
> *will humble themselves and*
> *pray, and seek my face,*
> *and turn from their wicked ways,*
> *THEN will I hear from heaven."*
> *2Chronicles 7:14*

When we try to 'go it alone', without prayer, we are not working with God. Prayer shifts us, aligns us, moves us and positions us with God…THEN GOD MOVES!

> *Prayer is not about moving God,*
> *prayer is about God moving us!*

All kinds of prayer

There are many ways to pray; petitions, intercessions, declarations, binding and loosing. The secret is to know what kind of prayer is needed to cause change and release in any given situation.

"With every prayer and petition,
pray at all times in the Spirit,
and to this end be alert, with all perseverance
and requests for all the saints."
Ephesians 6:18 NET

The apostle Paul listed three different kinds of prayer:-

1. "*Petitions*" - which are supplications or requests.

2. "*Intercessions*" - standing in the gap on behalf of someone else who is unable to pray.

3. "*Thanksgivings*" - the giving of thanks for things already received and to be received by faith.

"...(Abraham) was strengthened in his
faith as he gave glory to God."
Romans 4:20

Jesus taught **five** kinds of prayer:-

1. '*Forgiveness Prayer*' is the starting point - "*Forgive me*
my debts as I have also forgiven my debtors..." Matthew
6:12.

2. '*Binding Prayer*' - Matt 16:19

3. '*Loosing Prayer*' - Matt 16:19

4. '*Agreement Prayer*' - Matt 18:19

5. '*Creative Word Prayer*' - speaking into being, as an accomplished fact in faith, "*the things that be not as though they were*".

There comes a time in prayer when asking isn't enough, thanking isn't enough and intercession isn't enough. We must speak to our mountain, directly, creatively, faith-fully, Scripturally and authoritatively…we will have what we say!

> *"And Jesus answering said to*
> *them, Have faith in God.*
> *For truly I say to you, That whoever*
> *shall* **say** *to this mountain,*
> *Be removed, and be cast into the sea;*
> *and shall not doubt in his heart,*
> *but shall believe that those things*
> *which he* **says** *shall come to pass;*
> *he shall have whatever he* **says**.
> *Therefore I say to you,*
> *Whatever things you desire,*
> **when you pray**, *believe that you have*

received them, and you shall have them."
Mark 11:22-24

Carrying a burden of prayer

The apostle Paul also taught prayer as a 'travailing', or carrying a burden in prayer through to it's fulfillment.

"My little children, for whom I labour in
birth again until Christ is formed in you."
Galatians 4:19

Prayer priorities

Two priorities are to be at the top of the list in any corporate prayer meeting of the church:-

1. **Prayer for the Salvation of the lost**

*"Therefore I exhort **first of all***
that supplications, prayers, intercessions,
and giving of thanks be made for all men…
For this is good and acceptable in
the sight of God our Savior;
Who will have all men to be saved, and to
come unto the knowledge of the truth."

1Timothy 2:1,3,4
Prayer for government and peace

"For kings, and for all that are in authority;
that we may lead a quiet and peaceable
life in all godliness and honesty."
1Timothy 2:2

Chapter Seven

FINANCING THE LOCAL CHURCH

Two things are clear from a study of the history of the House of God in the Scriptures.

First, from the very beginning the House of God has always been God's provision of a "**storehouse**" for His people; a place of blessing, favor, prosperity and supply.

Second, all God's people from antiquity to the present day have willingly and generously supported God's House through the giving of "**tithes and offerings"** so the House of God would be 'self funding'.

Two great patriarchs set the example

Abraham, our "*father of faith*" (Romans 4:16), inaugurated tithing when he gave a "**tenth of all**" to Melchizedek the High Priest (Genesis 14:2.0).

The most important thing to realize is that this happened **before** the law was given. So how did Abraham arrive at the decision to tithe to the high priest?

The answer is found in Melchizedek's actions.

*"And Melchizedek king of Salem
brought forth bread and wine:
and he was the priest of the most high God.
And he blessed him, and said, Blessed
be Abram of the most high God,
possessor of heaven and earth:
And blessed be the most high God,
who has delivered your enemies into your hand.
And he gave him tithes of all."
Genesis 14:18-20*

Abraham received a twofold revelation from Melchizedek:-

- He **belonged to God**, "*the possessor of heaven and earth*", as God owns everything.

- He was "***blessed" by God",*** as God always blesses His people.

Therefore, Abraham responded in faith to that revelation by giving "*Him tithes of all*".

This is the essence of tithing. **Tithing is a faith response to a revelation of God's ownership of all things**, including myself, and, **that I am blessed by God.**

Jacob also received a revelation of God and the House of God at Bethel where he saw the House of God as the "*gate of heaven*".

From that moment Jacob responded in faith to his revelation by vowing that he would support the house of God through tithing and would serve God by building the House of God.

> *"And he called the name of that*
> *place Bethel (House of God)*
> *but the name of that city was*
> *called Luz at the first.*
> *And Jacob vowed a vow, saying,*
> *If God will be with me,*
> *and will keep me in this way that I go,*
> *and will give me bread to eat,*
> *and raiment to put on,*
> *So that I come again to my*
> *father's house in peace;*
> *then shall the Lord be my God:*
> *And this stone, which I have set for*
> *a pillar, shall be God's house:*

> *and of all that you shall give me I will*
> *surely give the tenth unto You."*
> *Genesis 28:19-22*

Tithing is all about recognizing and honoring God

Many Christians can miss the concept of tithing because of a failure to understand what tithing is really all about from God's viewpoint.

The concept of tithing is not just about a particular amount, that is 10%. Rather, tithing is all about recognizing and honoring God because He is "*the possessor of heaven and earth*".

The tithe is like God's signature on everything because God always reserves a part for Himself out of everything He makes!

The Principal of the Tithe:

> *God ALWAYS reserves a*
> *PART FOR HIMSELF*
> *out of EVERYTHING He makes*

The tithe is known in the Scriptures as the "*portion set apart for God*", which is considered to be "*Holy to the Lord*" (Exodus 28:38).

This was a common practice required by God throughout the Scriptures where God always reserves a portion for Himself out of everything he makes, but not necessarily called 'the Tithe', or 10%.

Once we understand this 'set apart' principle we can see tithing everywhere!

For example;:-

1. One Day set apart, one seventh (1/7), the Sabbath (Genesis 2:3)

2. One Tree set apart (1/60,000 species), the Tree of Knowledge of Good and Evil (Genesis 2:16-17)

3. The Firstborn set apart (Exodus 13:1-2)

4. One Tribe set apart, one twelfth (1/12), the Levites (Numbers 18:21)

5. The 1st city of conquest, Jericho, set apart (1/10 cities) (Joshua 6:2)

5. A Portion of the spoils of war set apart (Joshua 6:18,24)

6. The Nazarite set apart (Judah 13:4-5)

7. Honoring the Lord with first fruits ('tithe') set apart (Proverbs 3:9)

8. Christ as the first fruits ('tithe') of the resurrection set apart (1 Corinthians 15:23)

9. A Ministry, apostle, set apart (Acts 13:2)

10. The House of Stephanas as the *"first fruits of the Achaia"* ('tithe') set apart (1 Corinthians 16:15)

The tithe is the 'FIRST' of anything

The first recording of the 'principle of the tithe' is found in Genesis, where Abel *"brought of the **FIRSTBORN** of his flock and of their fat"*. God accepted his offering, but rejected his brother Cain's offering, which was just *"**AN** offering"* (Genesis 4:4).

The language used here is important because the Scriptures are making a distinction in the nature of the two offerings.

Abel's offering directly and specifically recognized the 'principle of the tithe', that is, the *"**FIRSTborn"**.* Whereas Cain's offering could be considered a 'general offering', that is, **AN offering",** that circumvented the 'principle of the tithe', which was to recognize and honor God with the first and the best!

Tithing in the New Testament

A commonly held view against tithing is that "*tithing is not in the New Testament*".

Of course, this is incorrect, as the word tithe and the principle of tithing is mentioned several times in the New Testament.

The first mention of Tithing in the New Testament is where Jesus commends the practice of Tithing alongside the matters of "*justice, mercy and faith*".

*"Woe unto you, scribes and
Pharisees, hypocrites!
for you pay tithe of mint and anise and cumin,
and have omitted the weightier matters
of the law, judgment, mercy, and faith:
these you ought to have done, and
not to leave the other undone."
Matthew 23:23*

The second mention of Tithing in the New Testament is where Luke also confirms this commendation of tithing by Jesus.

> *"But woe to you Pharisees! For*
> *you tithe mint and rue*
> *and all manner of herbs, and by pass*
> *justice and the love of God.*
> *These you ought to have done, without*
> *leaving the others undone.*
> *Luke 11:42*

The third mention of Tithing in the New Testament is found in the Epistle the Hebrews, where Tithing is mentioned **seven times** as part of Christ's High Priestly ministry as the New Testament Melchizedek (Hebrews 7:1-25).

The writer of Hebrews is comparing the earthly old covenant priesthood of Levi with the heavenly new covenant priesthood of Christ.

This shows the ways in which Christ's priesthood supersedes Levi's priesthood which represented the Old Covenant and law, because He is of the order of Melchizedek which based on "*resurrection life*" (Hebrews 7:16).

The conclusion:

Tithing is part of Christ's priesthood in the New Covenant

The fourth mention of tithing in the New Testament is found in the First Epistle to the Corinthians. The Apostle Paul is addressing wrong attitudes and complaints regarding the use of church finances for the support of it's ministers.

Paul refers to the Old Testament priesthood, showing that just as they lived from the Tithes and the Offerings of the temple (note that the words '*things*' and '*offerings*' which include all offerings, as in Numbers 18:19), so the '*Lord commands*' the same for the New Testament ministry.

> *"Do you not know that those who minister*
> *the **holy things** ('Tithes and*
> *Offerings') of the temple*
> *eat of the **things** of the temple*
> *('Tithes and Offerings'),*
> *and those who serve at the altar*
> *partake of the **offerings** of the altar*
> *('Tithes and Offerings')?"*
> *1 Corinthians 9:13*

The fifth mention of tithing in the New Testament is found in Matthew's Gospel, where Jesus equates Tithing to God with pay taxes to Caesar.

> *"Render unto Caesar the things*
> *that are Caesar's (Taxes),*
> *and to God the things that are God's (Tithes)."*
> *Matthew 22:21*

Tithing is an 'Eternal Principle'

There are certain 'eternal principles' in the economy of God. These 'eternal principles' are trans-dispensational, trans-covenantal principles that remain constant in God all the time.

Examples of 'eternal principles' which have always existed are faith, prayer, love and righteousness. Tithing is also an 'eternal principle' that has always existed throughout the Bible.

Tithing has always existed

Tithing was revealed at the time of the patriarchs, was included in the Law and the Prophets, and has continued in the Church Age.

The writer to the Hebrews confirms this when he observes that Abraham '*paid Tithes*' for himself before the Law, and for Levi, his offspring under the Law, and in fact, for all his future spiritual seed under the 'dispensation of grace'. (Galatians 3:29)

> *"Even Levi, who receives tithes,*
> *paid tithes through Abraham, so to speak,*
> *for he was still in the loins of his father*
> *when Melchizedek met him."*
> *Hebrews 7:9-10 (NKJV)*

SUMMARY OF TITHING THROUGHOUT THE BIBLE

Before the Law

1. Abel brings his first fruit (tithe') offering to God (Genesis 4:4)

2. Tithes paid by Abraham to Melchizedek, the High Priest (Genesis14:18-20)

3. Jacob vows to pay tithes to God (Genesis 28:16-22)

During the Law

4. Tithing instituted into the Mosaic Law
    (Leviticus 27:30-33)

5. The Tithe of the Tithes for Aaron and his Sons
    (Numbers 18:26-28)

6. The Tithes were Stored in the Temple, the House of
    God (Nehemiah 10:38-39, Malachi 3:10)

7. Tithes were withheld in times of revival

    a. Under Hezekiah (2Chronicles 31:5-10)

    b. Under Nehemiah (Nehemiah 13:10-13)

8. Tithes were withheld by Israel in times of backsliding
    (Nehemiah 13:10, Malachi 3:10, Amos 4:4)

After the Law – New Testament

9. Tithing was customary in New Testament times
    (Matthew 23:23, Luke 11:42; Luke 18:12)

10. Jesus commended and commanded the custom of
    Tithing (Matthew 22:21; 23:23)

11. Paul refers to and links giving to support church apostles and ministers with Old Testament tithing (1Corinthians 9:13-14)

12. Tithing is continued and incorporated in the High Priestly Ministry of the Lord Jesus Christ in the order of Melchizedek (Hebrews 7:1-17)

Tithing in the church today

One of the most common positions held today by many Christians, is as follows; "*I don't tithe because tithing is a law in the Old Testament and I'm not under the Law, I'm under grace in the New Testament.*"

This could be called 'the grace card', whereby Christians can exempt themselves from any responsibility of actually obeying the Scriptures!

Here's the thing: tithing, like every other New Testament practice and requirement, is never about obeying a law ("I HAVE to"), it is all about responding to a revelation ("I GET to")!

However, no matter how we look at this, the **BIG** problem with this mindset and position is that giving is not working in the present day church in the way that it was designed by God to work.

Let me explain.

The following statistics on the state of giving in the USA church, for example, bears this out.

*"On average Christians give 2.5%
of the income to churches.*

During the Great Depression, they gave 3.3%.

(Nonprofit Source, 2018, USA)

*"Tithers only make up 10-25%
of any congregation."*

(Nonprofit Source, 2018, USA)

*"Religious giving is down
about 50% since 1990."*

(New York Times, 2016)

The big elephant in the room that needs addressing is this; If "giving by grace" is so superior to "giving by law", as some suppose, how come giving is at such a low state in the church today?

It is simply naive and foolish to boldly state that one is superior under grace but is actually falling short of those who practice the law!

The average Israelite 'under the law' gave around 20-25% of their income to God in tithes and offerings, while many Christians today 'under grace' are struggling with giving God 10%!

Tithing was included in the law, not originated in the law

Just because tithing was included in the Law doesn't mean that tithing originated in the Law, or stopped after the law. This negates the concept that "tithing is a law".

Tithing preceded the Law in the Old Testament and supersedes the Law in the New Testament under grace! In other words, tithing 'under grace' goes far beyond tithing under the law.

The missing ingredient of the revelation of faith

The answer to this whole problem of giving is found in the missing ingredient of the '**revelation of faith**', for, "***The just shall live by faith***!" (Romans 1:17)

Our faith must have actions of obedience and not just remain as words, an idea or theory.

> *"Even so faith, if it has not works,*
> *it is dead, being alone.*
> *Yes, a man may say, You have*
> *faith, and I have works:*
> *show me your faith without your works,*
> *and I will show you my faith by my works."*
> *James 2:17-18*

Grace by itself is the right and power to act, but if grace isn't actioned and appropriated through faith it is dead and futile!

To live by faith means to live by revelation

To "live by faith" is a life of responding to and acting upon what has been revealed to me by the Holy Spirit, with no physical evidence. All the patriarchs tithed, not by a law (for the law didn't exist then), but by a revelation about God in their faith.

"Now faith is the substance of things hoped for,
the evidence of things not seen."
Hebrews 11:1

Trusting God in Tithing

To give God the "first fruits", or the tithe, **before** we see the provision, or if we'll have enough at the end of the month, takes faith!

Tithing takes a position of trusting God and saying to Him, "Lord, I'm putting You first in my life, and I'm trusting you for my financial needs."

Then we honor God by giving offerings out of our abundance!

Honoring God in Tithes and Offerings

It is clear from the Scriptures that Tithing is different from Offerings. Offerings are 'free will', that is, given willingly at the discretion of and according to the generosity of the giver.

> *"And the Lord spoke to Moses, saying,*
> *Speak to the children of Israel, that*
> *they bring me an offering:*
> *from everyone that gives it willingly with*
> *his heart you shall take my offering."*
> *Exodus 25:1-2*

> *"So let each one give as he*
> *purposes in his heart,*
> *not grudgingly, or of necessity;*
> *for God loves a cheerful giver. "*
> *2Corinthians 9:7*

The tithe, however, has **always** been *'the Lord's'* throughout all Biblical history.

> *"And all the tithe of the land,*
> *whether of the seed of the land, or of*
> *the fruit of the tree, **is the Lord's**:*
> ***it is holy to the Lord**."*
> *Leviticus 27:30*

The tithe belongs to the Lord

The tithe belongs to the Lord, therefore, the tithe is '**paid**' not '**given**'. We cannot give to God what He already owns!

The writer to the Hebrews explains that Levi, who was under the Law, "*paid tithes to Melchizedek through Abraham*". The only conclusion from this is that all are to pay tithes to Melchizedek, the Lord Jesus Christ.

> *"Even Levi, who receives tithes,*
> ***paid tithes*** *through Abraham…"*
> *Hebrews 7:9*

Supporters of 'non-tithing' cannot show any scripture that pronounces the cessation of the practice and principle of tithing. Nor can we draw a conclusion from minimal referencing to tithing in the New Testament - 'silence is not consent'!

Tithing in the New Testament is not to be practiced as a law

As Christians we would uphold the good and healthy practice of setting Sunday apart as a day of rest and worship, but not as a law. Therefore, it is not a sin for us to work, shop or play sport on a Sunday because we prioritize Sunday as a part of a good and healthy Christian lifestyle, but not as a rigid law keeping. Going to church will not save us!

Another example is the keeping of the Sabbath. While we do not keep the Sabbath as a law in the New Testament church, the principle of rest and rejuvenation is still understood today as beneficial. Most would agree that at least one day of the week dedicated to rest from work is healthy and wise. Most Judeo-Christian societies have provided a days rest from work for its citizens, Sunday.

Therefore, we also conclude that Tithing also is not to be practiced as a law in the New Testament church. Rather it should be an outworking of the revelation regarding the grace and goodness of God in our lives through faith.

> *"That the righteous requirements of*
> *the law might be fulfilled in us*
> *who do not walk according to the*
> *flesh but according to the Spirit."*
> *Romans 8:v4*

What about 'Spirit led giving'?

Another commonly held position about not needing to tithe is; "*I am lead by the Spirit, therefore, I don't need to tithe.*" If this statement was really true no church would never be short of funds!

This statement of course is true in the sense that the motive and actions of the New Covenant are not based on the works of law, but rather on the faith response to God's grace in our lives, being "led by the Spirit".

However, the Holy Spirit will never lead us away from the character, principles, commands or righteousness of God.

Therefore, if we are truly empowered and led by the Holy Spirit, our giving will not only fulfill the law, but will also supersede it!

*"Unless your righteousness exceeds
the righteousness of the scribes and Pharisees,
you will by no means enter the
kingdom of heaven."*
Matthew 5:20

While it is possible to 'be totally led by the Spirit' in

giving, the amount the Holy Spirit directs would never be less than the Tithe! Otherwise, the Holy Spirit would be disagreeing with the command and principle of the Word of God.

We conclude that there are two ways to give:-

First, *"tithe first, then decide how to give in offerings"*.

Or, Second, *"give as the Spirit leads"* and then use a calculator to to see if it really was the Holy Spirit leading you!" (more than the tithe)

> *The Tithe belongs to God BEFORE we give,*
> *The offerings belong to God AFTER we give*

Tithing Keeps Me Honest!

I have personally found that by starting 'my giving' with 10%, the Tithe, I am kept honest in my giving. That is, I am assured of never giving below what a Pharisee under the law would give!

> *The law is the measuring stick*
> *of my 'spirit led giving'…it keeps me honest!*

The true test of our righteousness is not what we think or feel, but what the law of God "*witnesses*" to, and gives as the standard.

> *"But now the righteousness of God
> apart from the law is revealed,
> being witnessed by the Law…"*
> *Romans 3:21*

Therefore, our giving, as Holy Spirit led and empowered believers will always exceed the standards of the Law! In other words, the grace of God is higher than the Law and super abounds over all the requirements of the Law. There is no law against the fruit (results) of the Spirit.

> *"But the fruit of the Spirit is…
> against such there is no law."*
> *Galatians 5:22-23*

The true test of "Spirit led giving" is this: if I calculate my actual giving over the last year, the total should exceed the tithe of my income!

To say that I am "led by the Spirit", and yet in reality fall short of 'pharisaical righteousness', I am insulting God's grace, and I am short-changing what it really means to be led by the Spirit of God.

> *"Little children, let no one deceive you.*
> *He who practices righteousness is righteous,*
> *just as He is righteous."*
> *1 John 3:7*

Tithing has to do with the Blessing of God

The most important thing to realize about Tithing is that there are specific promises from God directly connected with Tithing.

This is clearly recorded in the Scriptures showing the blessing of God in the lives of men and women who had a revelation on Tithing, especially Abraham, who is presented as our great example and "*Father of Faith*" in the New Covenant (Romans 4:1).

> *"For this Melchizedek, king of Salem,*
> *priest of the Most High God, who*
> *met Abraham returning from the slaughter*
> *of the kings and **blessed him...***
> *received tithes from Abraham and*
> ***blessed him who had the promises**.*

**Now beyond all contradiction the
lesser is blessed by the better.**"
Hebrews 7:1,6,-7

*"And prove me now in this, says the
Lord of Hosts, If I will not open the
windows of Heaven and* **pour out for
you such blessing** *that there will
not be room enough to receive it"*
Malachi 3:10-11

*"Honor the Lord with your possessions,
and the first fruits of all your increase;
So* **your barns will be filled with plenty,**
and **your vats will overflow with new wine**"
Proverbs 3:9-10

An example of the people of God losing the blessings of
God for not bringing their Tithes and Offerings into the
House of God is found in the days of Haggai the prophet.

Haggai's prophecy uses the same language as Malachi:-

"Consider your ways! You have

sown much, and bring in little;
You eat, but do not have enough…
and he who earns wages,
earns wages to put in a bag with
holes….you looked for much,
but indeed it came to little;
and when you brought it home, I blew it away.
WHY? Says the Lord of Hosts.
Because My House that is in ruins, while
everyone of you runs to his own house.
Therefore the heavens above you withhold
the dew, and the earth withholds it fruit…
and I will fill this temple with glory…

The silver is Mine, and the gold is
Mine, says the Lord of Hosts.
The glory of this latter temple shall
be greater than the former."
Haggai 1:5-11, 2:8-9

The Purpose of the Tithe

The purpose of the Tithe is clear; "*You shall not forsake the Levite who is within your gates, for he has no inheritance with you.*"(Deuteronomy 14:27)

The Tithe has always been God's way of funding the priesthood. Nothing has changed with God since the beginning.

God has always had a priesthood and He has always funded His priesthood through the Tithes given by His people.

TITHES ARE FOR THE 'MINISTRY OF THE HOUSE'

> *"..to whom Melchizedek also Abraham*
> *gave a tenth part of all…"*
> *Hebrews 7:2*

> *"For the tithes of the children of Israel,*
> *which they offer up as a heave*
> *offering to the Lord, I HAVE GIVEN TO*
> *THE LEVITES as an inheritance…"*
> *Numbers 18:24*

> *"…then you (Levites) shall offer up a*
> *heave offering of it to the Lord, a*
> *tenth of the tenth…and you shall*

> *give it to Aaron the priest."*
> *Numbers 18:26-28*

Before there was a 'temple', or 'church', Abraham paid his Tithes directly to Melchizedek, the High Priest.

Paul refers to this concept in his defense of his ministry to the Corinthians, who were complaining about money going to Paul and his team of ministers. Paul called the funding of the ministry through Tithes and Offerings "a right" (1Corinthians 9:3-6,12,14), not an option. He directly links the support of New Testament ministers to the Old Testament pictures of Tithes; the support of shepherds, farmers, soldiers, and of oxen treading out the grain (1Corinthians 9:7-12).

> *"Do you not know that those who*
> *minister the holy things eat of the*
> *things of the temple…even so the*
> *Lord has commanded that those*
> *who preach the gospel should*
> *live from the gospel."*
> *1Corinthians 9:13-14*

The Purposes of Offerings

OFFERINGS ARE FOR THE 'VISION OF THE HOUSE'

If the Tithes are to be used for the support of the ministry of the House of God, what are the Offerings to be used for?

Offerings were raised to fund the 'Vision of the House' of God which were to support the expansion activities of the House of God.

Offerings reach out way beyond the daily support of the priesthood in ministering to God and the people.

This is because there is always more 'vision' than 'ministry'. Vision by it's very nature stretches and extends way beyond current and usual needs and capabilities.

There is always more 'Vision' than 'Ministry'

The Israelites, therefore, were given many opportunities to give offerings both regularly, alongside the collection of the tithes, and spontaneously as they felt the need to give. They also gave in response to organized offerings arranged by the priests to meet special needs and projects as they arose.

The application of Offerings

The offerings in the Scriptures were used firstly **to cover the building expenses of the House of God**. Offerings covered the physical construction, repairs, maintenance and extensions of the House of God.

> *"Speak to the children of Israel, that*
> *they bring me an offering.*
> *From everyone who gives it willingly*
> *with his heart you shall take My*
> *offering...And let them make Me a*
> *sanctuary, that I may dwell among them."*
> *Exodus 25:2,8*

> *"Joash set his heart on repairing the*
> *house of the Lord...Go..and gather*
> *from all Israel money to repair*
> *the house of your God."*
> *2Chronicles 24:4-5*

Second, offerings were collected **for special needs**, such as the support of widows, and church members in times of famine and disaster.

"Then one of them, named Agabus,
stood up and showed by the Spirit that
there was going to be a great famine
throughout all the world which also
happened in the days of Claudius Caesar.
Then the disciples, each according to his ability,
determined to send relief to the
brethren dwelling in Judea.
Acts 11:28-29

The third purpose of offerings in the Scriptures was for **the support of missionary and outreach ministry.**

"Do you not know that those who
minister the holy things eat of the
things of the temple…even so the
Lord has commanded that those
who preach the gospel should
live from the gospel."
1Corinthians 9:13-14

This was common in the New Testament, where the missionary and church planting work of Paul and his associates, for example, were funded by the offerings from cooperating local churches and individuals.

"Did I commit sin in humbling myself
that you might be exalted,
because I preached the gospel of
God to you free of charge?
I robbed other Churches taking wages
from them to minister to you."
2Corinthians 11:7-8

Some churches like the church at Philippi, for example, gave regularly to Paul as a "*partnership*":-

"Now you Philippians know also that
in the beginning of the gospel,
when I departed from Macedonia,
no church shared with me concerning
giving and receiving, but you only.
*For even in Thessalonica **you sent aid***
***once and again** unto my necessities."*
Philippians 4:15-16

My personal financial journey

I started tithing as a result of simply doing what what my Pastors did…they tithed and so did I!

However, I had much to learn on my financial journey. I married quite young at 21 and my wife and I continued to tithe conscientiously and we 'got by'. We were always 'blessed' and had 'sufficient' in our finances, but looking back we were never in abundance.

This never bothered me because I was bought up with a good old blue colour work ethic, many times working two and three jobs on top of my teaching and later pastoral jobs to 'make ends meet'.

However, everything came to a critical point as our church in Brisbane began to grow and so did the financial demands grow with it. I was struggling with the 'always too much month and not enough money' syndrome.

One day in my pressured existence I began to pour out my complaint to the Lord!

"Why are we always struggling financially?" We tithe and don't seem to live prospered?"

Why is the church struggling financially?" "Why are wealthy people in our church not giving?!" "If they gave properly we would be ok!"

Then silence.

Then, the inner voice of the Holy Spirit spoke to me so clearly, "*You don't live by their giving, you live by your giving!*"

> "*You don't live by their giving,*
> *you live by your giving!*"

BOOM! A revelation moment!

I realized in that moment that I was 'a tither', but not 'a giver'!

To release financial abundance I needed 'to put faith seed into the ground'. Malachi prophesied that "tithes **AND** offerings" **working together** brought a "*not enough room to contain blessing*!

I had the tithing component, but not the offerings component.

Tithing creates the opportunity and the environment, Offerings create the harvest!

In that moment I responded to God, "OK God, with your help I want to be the biggest giver in our church!"

Then the journey began. Instead of looking to others to give, my wife and I committed ourselves to a lifestyle of giving; of sowing and reaping above and beyond tithing.

I began to read and study the Scriptures and devoured books on finance and wealth creation from everywhere. I arranged meetings with some of the millionaires I knew and asked them questions about money and asked them to coach me. No one refused me.

What surprised me was how financially illiterate I was! I discovered that in reality I was a poverty minded person who actually knew very little about money and how it worked. I needed to change and grow financially.

The power of revelation began to work in me. I began to tithe and give offerings in faith expecting a harvest. As a result, prosperity and abundance began to flow into our personal lives and into our church.

Things began to change very rapidly, especially how I preached on money. Instead of teaching, exhorting and appealing to people to give, I began to speak out from my person revelation regarding blessing, abundance, prosperity, money and giving.

My language changed from "*you need to give*", to, "*here's what I've discovered about giving!*"

As a result, our personal finances began to change and the church's income began to increase.

"Ministers in the marketplace"

We then added the theme of finances for the month of June every year. I began preaching and teaching from the Bible on finances, business and career, financial success and prosperity.

The highlight of the month was a 'BAS' Sunday, an acronym for "Business Anointing Sunday", in which I prayed for and anointed our business and professional people.

Our church began to intentionally 'commission' and send every member as 'ministers in the marketplace' to succeed and prosper and be witnesses of the grace and goodness of God to their colleagues and customers.

When I started BAS Sundays there was only a handful of business and professional people in our church. But that didn't worry me. I was motivated by a clear revelation and began to move ahead in faith.

After a few years we were praying for and anointing hundreds of business and profession people; male and female, young and old!

Then it happened. My wife and I were able to give the biggest offering into our church building fund. WOW! We were so excited.

But then, what happened next became the ongoing story of our church's finances.

The people who we were leading and mentoring began to prosper. So much so that we were soon overtaken by their levels of prosperity, offerings, overflow and generosity.

The amazing thing to observe was that many of them were younger members; succeeding in their careers, starting businesses, buying houses and prospering financially.

This was truly satisfying to be a part of. We were leading our church out of personal revelation and helping others to prosper and live their best life!

We discovered that God not only blesses us spiritually, but also physically and financially!

> *"Beloved, I pray above all things*
> *that you may prosper and be in health,*
> *even as your soul prospers."*
> *3John 2*

CHURCH - GATE OF HEAVEN

Chapter Eight

THE ENEMIES OF THE CHURCH

The Bible teaches us that we are engaged in a spiritual, invisible war taking place between the forces of God and the forces of the Devil.

The moment we are born again we are on God's side and the powers of darkness are immediately against us!

The Scriptures declare that God has fully prepared and equipped us for victory in Christ through two supernatural provisions:-

The full and finished work of Christ in defeating the devil at the cross and through His resurrection

> *"Blotting out the handwriting of*
> *ordinances that was against us,*
> *which was contrary to us, and took it*
> *out of the way, nailing it to his cross;*

*And having spoiled principalities and
powers, he made a show of them
openly, triumphing over them in it."
Colossians 2:14-15*

*"For this purpose the Son of
God was manifested,
that He might destroy the works of the devil."
1John 3:8*

The provision of spiritual armory to stand against the devil and his schemes

*"Put on the whole armor of God,
that you may be able to stand
against the wiles of the devil.
For we wrestle not against flesh and blood,
but against principalities, against powers,
against the rulers of the darkness of this world,
against spiritual wickedness in high places."
Ephesians 6:11-12*

This spiritual war began with the expulsion of the Devil from heaven because of his attempted rebellion against God.

"And there was war in heaven:
Michael and his angels fought
against the dragon;
and the dragon fought and his angels,
And prevailed not; neither was their
place found any more in heaven.
And the great dragon was cast out, that
old serpent, called the Devil, and Satan,
who deceives the whole world: he
was cast out into the earth,
and his angels were cast out with him."
Revelation 12:7-9

The effects of this spiritual war has had physical consequences for humans ever since.

It began with the temptation of Adam and Eve and their subsequent expulsion from the Garden of Eden and the presence of God. And it has been the ongoing source of contention and war ever since.

The plan and work of the Devil has always been to enforce the separation between God and mankind that occurred as a result of 'the fall'.

The Church is built in a climate of war

When the Lord Jesus announced His intention to "***build My church***", He prophesied that it would be built in an climate and atmosphere of war.

> *"And I say to you, That you are Peter,*
> *and upon this rock I will build My church;*
> *and the gates of hell shall not prevail against it.*
> *Matthew 16:18*

From the very beginning enemies have sought to pull down and destroy the church. But the Lord Jesus declared that, "***the gates of hell will not prevail against it!***"

> *"For though we walk in the flesh,*
> *we do not war after the flesh:*
> *(For the weapons of our warfare are not carnal,*
> *but mighty through God to the*
> *pulling down of strong holds;)*
> *Casting down imaginations, and every high thing*
> *that exalts itself against the knowledge of God,*
> *and bringing into captivity every thought*
> *to the obedience of Christ."*
> *2Corinthians 10:3-5*

So what, or who, are the enemies of the church?

1. Enemies from WITHOUT

It is clear from the very beginning that the devil, or Satan, is the church's number one enemy, along with his hordes of demons.

The Lord Jesus was referring to this spiritual conflict when He said that the "*gates of hell*" wouldn't prevail against His church!

> *"Wherein in time past you walked*
> *according to the **course of this world**,*
> *according to the **prince of the power of the air**,*
> ***the spirit that now works in the***
> ***children of disobedience**:*
> *Among whom also we all had our conversation*
> *in times past in the **lusts of our flesh**, fulfilling*
> *the desires of the flesh and of the mind;*
> *and were by nature the children*
> *of wrath, even as others."*
> *Eph 2:2-3*

The second external enemy of the church is termed "The World", referring to the system of the world. This concept comes from the Greek word "*cosmos*", referring to the order of things, or as the apostle Paul framed it, "*the spirit that now works in the children of disobedience*" *(Ephesians 2:2).*

> *"Love not the world, neither the*
> *things that are in the world.*
> *If any man love the world, the love*
> *of the Father is not in him.*
> *For all that is in the world, the lust of*
> *the flesh, and the lust of the eyes,*
> *and the pride of life, is not of the*
> *Father, but is of the world.*
> *And the world passes away, and the lust thereof:*
> *but he who does the will of*
> *God abides for ever."*
> *1John 2:15-17*

The apostle John concluded that the whole world was living under the power and influence of the devil, the evil one.

> *"We know [for a fact] that we are of God,*
> *and the whole world [around us]*
> **lies in the power of the evil one**
> **[opposing God and His precepts]."**
> *1 John 5:19 (AMP)*

The most pernicious thing about this reality is that most people are blinded to this fact, because the devil has blinded them!

Therefore, the devil works covertly and secretly in the darkness of ignorance and unbelief in order to sabotage the church and the preaching of the gospel.

> *"But if our gospel be hid, it is*
> *hid to them that are lost:*
> *In whom* **the god of this world has blinded**
> **the minds of them which believe not**,
> *lest the light of the glorious gospel of Christ,*
> *who is the image of God, should*
> *shine unto them."*
> *2Corinthians 4:3-4*

The thief, the wolf and the the hireling

*"The **thief** does not come except to*
steal, and to kill, and to destroy:
I have come that they may have life, and
that they might have it more abundantly.
I am the good shepherd: the good
shepherd gives His life for the sheep.
*But a **hireling**, he who is not the shepherd,*
one who does not own the sheep,
*sees the **wolf** coming, and leaves*
the sheep and flees;
and the wolf catches the sheep
and scatters them.
The hireling flees because he is a hireling
and does not care about the sheep."
John 10:10-13

The "**thief**" is an arch enemy of the church because their methods are simple; to steal, kill and destroy God's people.

Jesus is figuratively referring to false prophets and false teachers who seek to rob His people of truth and stealing people's ability to see spiritually and enter salvation.

The "**hireling**", however, is a much more subtle enemy because they come from the outside pretending to care for God's people, His sheep. The hireling is only after financial reward.

As a result the hireling brings destruction to the church because a hireling will not protect what he does not 'own'.

Therefore, the hireling is a counterfeit shepherd, or pastor, who will not protect the flock of God from the "**wolf**". As a result, the wolf finds it easier to attack the vulnerable and the young of the church.

The wolf "*catches*" sheep and "*scatters*" the flock. These two works of the wolf are to be countered by the "*good shepherd*", who lays down his life for the sheep and stops the wolf from catching and scattering God's people.

2. Enemies from WITHIN

One would think that the church would be kept sufficiently busy just countering the attacks of the devil from without. However, this is far from the reality, as the church has had to deal with enemies from within it's own ranks from the very beginning!

As the apostle Paul declared with weeping;

> *"Brethren, join in following my example,*
> *and note those who so walk, as*
> *you have us for a pattern*
> *For many walk, of whom I have told you*
> *often, and now tell you even weeping,*
> **that they are the enemies of**
> **the cross of Christ:**
> *Whose end is destruction,*
> *whose god is their belly,*
> *and whose glory is in their shame*
> *- who mind earthly things."*
> *Philippians 3:17-19*

"Many antichrists have come"

The apostle John also referred to these individuals as *"antichrists"*, who were once part of the church and were now part of the devil's work in the pulling down and destroying the church by their words and actions!

The total destruction and even the hatred of the church, the chosen of God, is the goal and the spirit of antichrist.

> *"Little children, it is the last hour: and as you*

have heard that the Antichrist is coming,
even now many antichrists have come,
by which we know that it is the last hour.
**They went out from us, but
they were not of us**;
*for if they had been of us, they
would have continued with us:
but they went out that they
might be made manifest,
that none of them were of us."
1John 2:18-19*

Divisions and *"party spirit"*

From the very beginning of the church there has always been the human tendency to make heroes of people and follow them rather than following Christ.

The apostle Paul needed to correct this kind of division in the Corinthian church and even had a group pro-porting to "follow Christ"!

Paul's instruction was clear: we must resist our carnality, human tendencies and preferences, when it comes to the church of God. We are called to be followers of the Lord Jesus Christ not people.

> *"For you are still carnal:*
> *For where there is envy, strife,*
> *and divisions among you,*
> *are you not carnal, and behaving like mere men?*
> *For when one says, "I am of Paul"; and another,*
> *"I am of Apollos"; are you not carnal?*
> *Who then is Paul, and who is Apollos,*
> *but ministers through whom you believed,*
> *as the Lord gave to each one?*
> *I have planted, Apollos watered;*
> *but God gave the increase.*
> *So then, neither is he who plants is*
> *anything, nor he who waters;*
> *but God who gives the increase."*
> *1Corinthians 3:3-7*

False doctrines and false prophets

One of the chief responsibilities of the leaders of the church is to be unified in the faith and doctrine of Christ. This enables the leaders to be able to correct false doctrines and teachings that arise from time to time in the church.

The apostle Paul stated this to the Ephesians as the role of leadership. The goal being the "***maturity of the saints***" in Christ.

"And he gave some, apostles;
and some, prophets;
and some, evangelists; and some,
pastors and teachers;
For the perfecting (adjusting) of the
saints*, for the work of the ministry,*
for the edifying of the body of Christ:
Till we all come in the unity of the faith, and
of the knowledge of the Son of God,
unto a perfect man, unto the measure of
the stature of the fulness of Christ:
That we henceforth be no more children,
tossed to and fro, and carried about
with every wind of doctrine*,*
by the sleight of men, and cunning craftiness,
whereby they lie in wait to deceive;
But speaking the truth in love*, may*
grow up into him in all things,
which is the head, even Christ."
Ephesians 4:11

Competing and rival visions

The vision, calling and blueprint of every local church is located in the heart of the founding, apostolic person. It is through the *"obedience to heavenly vision"* that a local church discovers its true meaning and fulfillment.

As the church grows and develops, however, other leaders and ministries can arise who feel that they have a right to bring about a change to a 'far better vision and calling' than the original and existing one - theirs! This can be the cause of so much conflict and division in a church because these rival visions tend to drain the energy and focus of the church and its leaders.

Therefore, one of the key roles of the senior leader, the pastoral team and the board of a local church is to protect the integrity of the founding vision, values and calling of the church.

Founding apostle 'rights'

The founding apostle of a church has 'founding rights' over all other leaders. The apostle Paul exercised these 'founding rights' referring to them as *"the grace of God given to me as a wise master-builder"*.

Paul understood that other leaders coming after him were to *"build upon"* the foundation laid by him, not *"change it"*!

*"**According to the grace of God which is
given unto me, as a wise master-builder**,
I have laid the foundation, and
another builds upon it.
But let every man take heed
how he builds upon it."
1Corinthians 3:10*

Paul encouraged the Corinthians not receive anyone who preached a different Jesus, a different message, or brought a different spirit other than what he had delivered to them as their founding apostle.

*"For if he who comes and preaches another
Jesus whom we have not preached,
or if you receive a different spirit, which you
have not received, or different gospel,
which you have not accepted - you
may well put up with it!
For I consider that I am not at all inferior
to the most eminent apostles."
2Corinthians 11:4-5*

Opinions

One of the biggest enemies of the church today would

be opinion, especially in this social media generation, where everyone has an opinion and everyone's opinion is considered as fact!

Another feature arising from this phenomenon is the recognition of "*Influencers*", who derive this status from the number of '*friends and followers*' and '*likes*' they accumulate. This is all achieved without qualification, accreditation or examination!

However, opinions without experience and expertise are just that, opinions!

Even the apostle Paul had to deal with this, so he took a position of keeping his opinions to himself and only speaking of the things that "*Christ had accomplished through me, in word and deed*".

In other words, he made it his aim to stick to his experience and expertise, not opinion, or someone else's foundation.

> *"For I will not dare to speak*
> *of any of those things*
> *which Christ has not accomplished*
> *through me, in word and deed,*
> *to make the Gentiles obedient -*
> *in mighty signs and wonders, by the*

power of the Spirit of God;
so that from Jerusalem and round
about unto Illyricum,
I have fully preached the gospel of Christ.
And so I have made it my aim to preach the
gospel, not where Christ was named,
lest I should build on another man's foundation."
Romans 15:18-20

Chapter Nine

THE POWER OF PLACEMENT
IN THE LOCAL CHURCH

*"**God sets the solitary in families**:*
He brings out those who are
bound into prosperity;
But the rebellious dwell in a dry land."
Psalms 68:6

The miracle of the new birth in Christ removes our sin, our past and our old life, creates a totally new person in Christ and places us instantly into the family of God.

No one would ever think of leaving their new born child at the hospital or with a stranger. Rather, the child is brought home and welcomed with joy and celebration into their family.

So it is with us spiritually. When we are born again we are welcomed with joy and celebration into our spiritual family and home, our local church.

> *"And the Lord **added to the church** daily*
> *those who were being saved."*
> *Acts 2:47*

We are 'born' or 'adopted' into our local church family

Being born into our church family is the common experience of every believer. The Psalm of the sons of Korah spoke of this in their song of Mount Zion and Jerusalem, declaring, *"This one and that one were born in her."*

> *"His foundation is in the holy mountains.*
> *The Lord loves the gates of Zion*
> *more than the dwellings of Jacob.*
> *Glorious things are spoken of you,*
> *O city of God! Selah*
> *"I will make mention of Rahab and*
> *Babylon to those who know Me.*
> *Behold, O Philistia and Tyre, with Ethiopia.*
> *'This one was born there.'"*
> *And of Zion it will be said,*

*"**This one and that one were born in her;***
and the Most High shall establish her."
The Lord will record, when He
registers the people's:
*"**This one was born there**." Selah*
Both the singers and players on instruments say,
"All my springs are in you."
Psalms 87:1-7

Mount Zion is where the capital city of Jerusalem is located until this day. In the Old Testament Jerusalem was the 'natural city', or earthly city, of the people of Israel.

In the New Testament the new Jerusalem is the 'spiritual city', or heavenly city, of the church, the people of God.

"But you have come unto Mount Zion
and to the city of the living God,
the heavenly Jerusalem, and to an
innumerable company of angels,
To the general assembly and church of the
firstborn, who are registered in heaven,
to God the Judge of all, to the spirits
of just men made perfect,
to Jesus the Mediator of the new covenant,
and to the blood of sprinkling that speaks
better things than that of Abel."
Hebrews 12:22-24

However, in contemporary society where population movement and migration has been increasing, a new phenomenon of being 'adopted' into a local church from 'outside', or from another church, is occurring more and more.

So, whether we are 'born' or 'adopted' into our local church family, the most important thing is that we find our local church home. We were not meant to do our Christian faith alone. God has always intended that we would live out our faith in the context of community.

> *"Now therefore you are no longer*
> *strangers and foreigners,*
> *but fellow citizens with the saints,*
> *and of the household of God;*
> *And are built upon the foundation*
> *of the apostles and prophets,*
> *Jesus Christ Himself being the*
> *chief corner stone;*
> *In Whom all the building fitly framed together*
> *grows unto a holy temple in the Lord:*
> *In whom you also are builded together for*
> *an habitation of God through the Spirit."*
> *Ephesians* 2:19-22

The apostle Paul defined the experience of the new birth as the "*baptism into one body*".

> *"For by one Spirit we were all*
> **baptized into one body,**
> *whether we be Jews or Gentiles - whether*
> *Jews or Greeks, whether slaves or free -*
> *and have all been made to drink into one Spirit."*
> *1Corinthians 12:13*

He also directly linked the receiving of spiritual gifts, through the baptism of the Holy Spirit with God setting every believer in their place in the local church. Our giftings are not only linked to our place in the local church but to our function and contribution as a member of the body of Christ.

> *"But now* **God has set the members,**
> *each one of them,*
> *in the body just as He pleased.*
> *And if they were all one member,*
> *where would the body be?*
> *But now indeed there are many*
> *members, yet one body.*
> *And the eye cannot say to the*
> *hand, "I have no need of you;*

nor again the head to the feet,
"I have no need of you"."
1Corinthians 12:18-21

*"And **God has set some in the church**,*
first apostles, secondarily prophets,
thirdly teachers, after that miracles,
then gifts of healings, helps, governments,
diversities of tongues."
1Corinthians 12:28

Going TO church verses being placed IN church

This view of the local church and its members as a community of *"set"*, or placed, believers lifts the importance of identifying with our particular local church family.

We are not to be 'church goers', we are called, set and placed in the local church to BE THE CHURCH!

The problem of being found out of place

You may have heard it said, *"I don't have to go to church*

to be a Christian." Of course, this statement is totally ludicrous because it is a direct contradiction to the teaching of the New Testament.

It is better to be expressed this way; "*You don't have to be in church to find God because He can be found anywhere. But you do need to be in church to be a healthy Christian and find your place and your purpose.*"

"And let us consider one another
to provoke unto love and to good works:
Not forsaking the assembling
of ourselves together,
as the manner of some is;
but exhorting one another:
and so much the more,
as you see the day approaching."
Hebrews 10:24-25

The apostle Paul addressed this issue of being 'out of place' to the Corinthians by using the analogy of the body:-

"For the body is not one member, but many.
If the foot shall say, Because I am not
the hand, I am not of the body;

> *is it therefore not of the body?*
> *And if the ear shall say, Because I am*
> *not the eye, **I am not of the body**;*
> *is it therefore not of the body?*
> *If the whole body were an eye,*
> *where were the hearing?*
> *If the whole were hearing, where*
> *were the smelling?*
> ***But now has God set the members***
> ***every one of them in the body,***
> ***as it has pleased Him**."*
> *1Corinthians 12:14-18*

It is concerning and sad to hear any Christian declare their lack of need for the local church. Here's the thing: we need each other! We are better together!

> *"But now are they many members,*
> *yet but one body.*
> *And the eye cannot say unto the*
> *hand, I have no need of you:*
> *nor again the head to the feet,*
> *I have no need of you."*
> *1Corinthians 12:20-21*

No member of our natural body can function on it's own. Our fingers, for example, cannot exist and function in a healthy way without the hand and the hand without the arm and the arm without the shoulder. This is because the life, nourishment and health of the body flows from one member to another. Every member is practically and vitally linked.

So it is with the body of Christ. We find the place of spiritual health and purpose when we 'find our fit', or place, within the body of Christ, our local church family.

When we fail to find our home and place in God's House we can become spiritual wanderers, or vagabonds. The word vagabond means "*wandering from place to place without any settled home; nomadic*" (dictionary.com).

> *"As a bird that wanders from her nest,*
> *so is a man that wanders from his place."*
> *Proverbs 27:8*

When we become dislocated from our spiritual home we will find ourselves in a very vulnerable position. As a result we will be disconnected from the spiritual life, nourishment and support that flows from Christ through His body, the church.

God supplies His life, virtue, health and blessings through the "***joints***" (members joined together) and "***ligaments***" (the bonds of love and commitment) of the body, the local church. Simply put; God works through His people, the church.

> *"and not holding firmly to the Head,*
> ***from whom all the body,***
> ***being supplied and knit together***
> ***through the joints and ligaments,***
> *grows with God's growth."*
> *Colossians 2:19 WEB*

Connection language in the Bible

The language of the Bible is very precise when describing our connection to Christ and the church. This practical and vital connection to the local church is described as being; "*Abiding*", "*Joined*", "*Built*", "*Set*" and "*Born*".

Every believer is viewed as being simultaneously joined to Christ and His church when they are born again to become:-

- Branches *abiding* in the vine (John 15:5)
- Members *Joined* to the body (Ephesians 4:16)

- Living stones *built* into the house of God (1Peter 2:5)

- Members *set* in the body (1Corinthians 12:28)

- Children *born* into the family of God (John 1:12-13)

Joined to Christ equals joined to Church

The New Testament equates being joined to Christ as being joined to His church. Therefore, we cannot be joined to Christ and not be joined to His church!

Early church fathers like Cyprian also understood this truth.

> *"No one can have God for his Father,*
> *who has not the Church for his mother."*
> *Saint Cyprian of Carthage (190-258AD)*

Christians out of church?

Why are so many believers, who profess to be Christians, out of church today?

There can be many reasons, some understandable, but most invalid from God's viewpoint.

However, whatever the reason, the outcomes are not beneficial for those who are out of church connection.

Some of the reasons why professing Christians choose to be out of church are:-

Sin and non-Biblical lifestyles

First and foremost, some Christians choose to be out of church because they are practicing sins and non-Biblical lifestyles. As a result they reject 'church' and especially other Christians and leaders who are perceived as "judging them".

Regarding the "judging" of sin within the church. The New Testament instructs the church to "judge" its members "inside" the church who are sinning, but not unbelievers "outside" the church.

> *"But now I have written to you not to keep company with anyone named a brother, who is sexually immoral, or covetous, or an idolater, or a reviler, or a drunkard, or an extortioner - not even to eat with such a person.*

For what have I to do with judging
those who are outside?
Do you not judge those who are inside?
But those who are outside God judges.
Therefore "put away from
yourselves the evil person."
1Corinthians 5:11-12

The New Testament gives very clear instructions regarding sin and the effects of sin on the believer and the church.

For example, the apostle Paul makes it clear that those who habitually and continually practice sinning will forfeit their inheritance in the kingdom of God.

"Now the works of the flesh
are evident, which are;
Adultery, fornication, uncleanness, lewdness,
Idolatry, sorcery, hatred, contentions, jealousies,
outbursts of wrath, selfish ambitions,
dissensions, heresies,
Envy, murders, drunkenness,
revelries, and such like;
of the which I tell you beforehand, just
as I have also told you in time past,
*that **those who practice such things will***

not inherit the kingdom of God."
Galatians 5:19-21

The presence of sin in our lives is likened to a darkness that possesses our souls. The apostle John declares that when we are practicing sin we are reluctant to "*come to the light*" because our deeds will be exposed as "*evil*".

> *"And this is the condemnation, that*
> *the light has come into the world,*
> *and men loved darkness rather than*
> *light, because their deeds were evil.*
> *For everyone practicing evil hates the*
> *light, and does not come to the light,*
> *lest his deeds should be exposed,*
> *But he who does truth comes to the light,*
> *that his deeds may be clearly seen,*
> *that they have been done in God."*
> *John 3:19-21*

The Solution: Walking in the cleansing light of fellowship

The apostle John in his epistle declares that one of the major answers to overcoming sin is walking in the 'cleansing light of fellowship'.

It is through the "*fellowship with one another*" that the cleansing power of the blood of Christ actively "*cleanses us from all sin*". This is how important connection and fellowship in the church is!

> *"But if we walk in the light, as he is in the light,*
> *we have fellowship one with another,*
> *and the blood of Jesus Christ his*
> *Son cleanses us from all sin."*
> *1John 1:7*

Unresolved offenses

Second, some Christians choose to be out of church because they are carrying unresolved offense(s) in their hearts towards 'the church' and other Christians.

The result of this unforgiveness is often a rejection of church and especially other Christians because they have "hurt them".

The Lord Jesus Christ predicted that offenses would increase in the world, especially in the Last Days, causing betrayal and hatred to fill peoples hearts for others.

"And then shall many be offended,
and shall betray one another,
and shall hate one another."
Matthew 24:10

The Solution: Forgiveness

Our Lord Jesus Christ was very clear about the need for us to forgive others. God will withhold forgiveness from the unforgiving!

"And forgive us our debts, as
we forgive our debtors...
For if you forgive men their trespasses,
your heavenly Father will also forgive you:
But if you do not forgive men their trespasses,
neither will your Father forgive your trespasses."
Matthew 6:12, 14-15

The big question often asked then is; "Is my hurt justified?"

Emphatically yes, if an offense has been committed! People can act wrongly toward others and as a result people do get hurt.

However, Biblically, unforgiveness is never justified!

"But what if the offender isn't sorry?", one might protest.

> *Forgiveness frees the 'forgiver',*
> *repentance frees the 'offender'*

Here's the thing: repentance only works for a 'repentant offender', while forgiveness works for a 'forgiver'!

In other words, we don't need someone to be sorry and apologize for the power of forgiveness to work in us!

Forgiveness frees the offended at the point of forgiveness, while repentance frees the offender at the point of repentance.

In our journey of life there will always be offenses and some may never be resolved.

However, life is never about not being offended and hurt. Life is all about rising above our offenses and hurts through the power of forgiveness so we will be living a free and abundant life in Christ.

One of the dangers of unforgiveness is the practice of

'taking sides', where people not involved in a particular issue take up the offense of another. This is how a *"root of bitterness springs up and causes trouble, and by this many become defiled."* (Hebrews 12:15)

Three levels of living

There are three ways, or levels, to live our lives in regard to offenses and forgiveness:-

We can live '**OFFENDED**' - living constantly offended by everyone and everything

We can live '**FORGIVING**' - forgiving all our offenses by everyone and everything

We can live **'UNOFFENDABLE**' - deciding to not be offended by anyone or anything! And if we are offended, we have already decided to forgive immediately!

> *"And blessed is he, whoever shall*
> *not be offended in me."*
> *Matthew 11:6*

Faulty beliefs and unscriptural views

Third, Christians can choose to be out of church because

they have embraced unscriptural views and doctrines of Christ and His church. As a result the revelation of the importance, centrality and value of the church is eroded. This is without the balanced view of their church community.

One of the biggest dangers besetting the church today in regards to doctrine is the access to the internet by Christians. Now, while there are some benefits of the internet and social media, the problem can arise when individual Christians begin to entertain and embrace doctrines, beliefs and opinions by themselves on social media.

This is too often at the behest of unproven and complete strangers teaching, preaching and promoting their doctrines, beliefs, conspiracies and issues on the internet and social media platforms.

The Solution: Stay in a believing community

However, the Scriptural way to establish doctrinal belief is always in the context of the local church with the instruction and guidance of known, trusted and proven apostles, prophets, teachers and pastors, or leaders.

> *"Remember those who rule over you,*
> *who have spoken the word of God to you:*
> *whose faith follow, considering the*
> *outcome of their conduct."*
> *Hebrews 13:7*

"WE have the mind of Christ"

The "*mind of Christ*" is known in the "WE" (the church), not the "ME" (the individual)!

> *"For who hath known the mind of the*
> *Lord, that he may instruct him?*
> *But we have the mind of Christ."*
> *1Corinthians 2:16*

The importance of testing Outcomes or fruit

The reason why it is so important to receive teaching and doctrine from known and proven local church leaders is the ability to link actual outcomes, results, or fruit, with the teaching and doctrine.

In other words, have they lived it? Do they practice what they preach? Does it actually work in real life? What is the outcome or fruit of their teaching and doctrine?

The problem with so called social media "Influencers" is that there is no way to actually test and know their fruit. The number of 'likes' and 'followers' they have is not a "test of fruit", their lives are!

"Beware of false prophets, who come
to you in sheep's clothing,
but inwardly they are ravening wolves.
You will know them by their fruits.
Do men gather grapes of
thorns, or figs of thistles?
Even so every good tree brings forth good fruit;
but a corrupt tree brings forth evil fruit.
A good tree cannot bring forth evil fruit,
neither can a corrupt tree
bring forth good fruit."
Matthew 7:15-18

The apostle Paul encouraged Timothy to not listen to strangers, but rather, to continue in the "*traditions*" that he had received directly from Paul and his other pastors and leaders.

"You therefore, my son, be strong in the grace that is in Christ Jesus.

*And the things that you have heard
from me among many witnesses,
commit these to faithful men, who will
be able to teach others also."
2Tim 2:1-2*

These "*traditions*" and teachings were established "*among many witnesses*" by Paul and the apostles. This is known as the "***apostles doctrine***", which was personally given by Jesus Christ to the apostles and recorded as the New Testament Scriptures.

This is why the New Testament Scriptures, along with the Old Testament, are so important in the establishment of doctrine because they clearly present the "*apostles doctrine*" for all time.

*"And that from childhood you have
known the Holy Scriptures,
which are able to make you wise for salvation
through faith which is in Christ Jesus.
All scripture is given by inspiration of God,
and is profitable for doctrine, for reproof, for
correction, for instruction in righteousness:
That the man of God may be complete,
throughly equipped for every good work."
2Timothy 3:15-17*

Knowing your teachers

Paul makes it clear to Timothy that *"knowing from whom you have learned"* is essential to discovering and maintaining a bonafide Christian life grounded in the truth of the gospel of Christ.

> *"But you must continue in the things which you have learned and have been assured of,*
> **knowing from whom you have have learned them.***"*
> *2Timothy 3:13-17*

"What's in it for me?"

Fourth, some Christians can choose to be out of church because they believe the church does not meet their needs, desires and expectations; "what's in it for me!"

As a result, they find themselves unhappy with every and any local church, not realizing that the church doesn't exist for them, the church exists for the Lord Jesus Christ!

"For from Him, and through Him, and to Him, are all things:

to whom be glory for ever. Amen."
Romans 11:36

The moment we believe in Jesus Christ as our savior and lord we become His servants. From that moment we are called to live for Him and not for ourselves.

"For the love of Christ compels us;
because we judge thus: that if One
died for all, then all died:
And He died for all, that those who live
should live no longer for themselves,
but for Him who died for them, and rose again."
2Corinthians 5:14-15

The Solution: Live as servants of Christ

God has called us to a life of servanthood; living to serve Christ and others.

"For you, brethren, have been called to liberty;
only do not use liberty as an
opportunity for the flesh,
but through love serve one another."
Galatians 5:1

This servant attitude never considers "what's in it for me", or, "I don't get anything out of this". Instead, the servant of Christ is looking to see others encouraged, built up and blessed. The priority and focus is on being a contributor not a consumer in the house of God.

The Solution: Reassess our priorities

Fifth, Christians today can choose to be out of church, not because they don't want to be in church, but rather, they have accepted the attitude of the present world to make priorities and commitments with their time ahead of a commitment to the House of God. As a result, they find themselves "too busy" to be actively and regularly involved in church life.

This present secular world does not prioritize the importance of the house of God. Therefore, it should not be surprising that we find an ever increasing plethora of activities and opportunities, not evil in themselves, constantly being presented on Sunday, "*The Lord's Day*" (Revelation 1:10)

What should be our approach to this? Sunday worship is not a law, but rather a practice that Christians have been committed to since the beginning of the church.

The purpose of gathering together on a Sunday (the day Christ rose from the dead) is to commemorate Christ's death and resurrection and to be together for worship, teaching, fellowship and mutual encouragement.

This tradition was then later adopted by the Judeo-Christian world as a day off from work to attend church and participate in the hospitality and fellowship of the church.

However, as the West has grown increasingly secular and individualistic the importance of church and community has diminished greatly.

> *"Now on the first day of the week (Sunday),*
> *when the disciples came*
> *together to break bread,*
> *Paul, read to depart the next day,*
> *spoke to them and continued his*
> *message until midnight."*
> *Acts 20:7*

> *"On the first day of the week (Sunday)*
> *let each one of you lay something aside,*

storing up as he may prosper,
that there be no collections when I come."
1Corinthians 16:2

The Solution: Maturing in love

Sixth, some Christians can choose to be out of church because they have embraced a perfectionist view of the church. This can lead to seeing and amplifying the faults and lacks in the church, rather than appreciating the good things that actually exist and are happening in the church!

However, because we live in a state of imperfection until Jesus comes again, the perfect church does not exist.

"For we know in part, and we prophesy in part.
But when that which is perfect is come, then
that which is in part shall be done away.
When I was a child, I spake as a child, I
understood as a child, I thought as a child:
but when I became a man, I put
away childish things.
For now we see through a glass,
darkly; but then face to face:
now I know in part; but then shall I
know even as also I am known.

And now abides faith, hope, love, these three;
but the greatest of these is love. "
1Corinthians 13:9-13

'Issue driven Christians'

Seventh, Christians can choose to be out of church because they are focussing on one issue, or one aspect of the gospel, at the expense of *"all the counsel of God"* (Acts 20:27).

This myopic, narrow minded view of the church and the gospel inevitably leads to a separation and a division from the church. This is because, *"the church is not doing anything about this*!" The important questions to ask are, "what is the church's mission?" What is the church called to focus on?

It is important to 'live on mission' rather than spending energy and time on side issues that do not promote and help fulfill the mission and purposes of the church.

The Solution: Keeping the main game the main game

It is so important in this issue driven, 'lobbyist age', where so many are caught up in divisive issues that the church does not get caught up in such controversies. But rather, the church must stay focused on the preaching of the gospel to win lost people and make disciples and the building up of the church.

The apostle Paul put is this way:-

> *"For I determined not to know*
> *any thing among you,*
> *except Jesus Christ and Him crucified.*
> *And my speech and my preaching were not*
> *with persuasive words of human wisdom,*
> *but in demonstration of the Spirit and of power,*
> *that your faith should not be*
> *in the wisdom of men,*
> *but in the power of God."*
> *1Corinthians 2:2,4-5*

The church exists to "*declare the testimony of God*" and to be "*ambassadors for Christ*", not political or social ambassadors!

> *"Now then, we are ambassadors for Christ,*
> *as though God were pleading through us:*
> *we implore you on Christ's behalf,*

be reconciled to God."
2Corinthians 5:20

Wanting a significant voice

Eighth, one observation I have made over many years is that some Christians can choose to be out of church because they have not been given a significant voice and influence in the direction, nature and decision making of church.

This tends to happen when individuals have a higher opinion of their gifts and role in the church than they ought to. Sometimes this can even lead to an attitude of judgement and criticism which seeks to bring correction and adjustment to the church.

However, in a healthy, growing church this is not the reality. Every church must move beyond the situation where "everyone is INVOLVED", "everyone is INFORMED" and "everyone is an INFLUENCE".

The Solution: We must find our place

Every member of the church will 'find their place' when

they understand their gifts and role in the church and get busy with their particular contribution to build up the church.

This is why "knowing our place in the scheme of things" is so important because we all have different gifts, roles and "*functions*" in the church.

> *"For I say, through the grace given to*
> *me, to everyone who is among you,*
> *not to think of himself more highly than*
> *he ought to think; but to think soberly,*
> *as God has dealt to each one a measure of faith.*
> *For as we have many members in one body,*
> *but all members do not have the same function."*
> *Romans 12:3-4*

Planted Christians flourish

How different the picture looks for those who are planted in God's house. They flourish and grow!

> *"The righteous shall flourish like a palm tree*
> *and grow like a cedar in Lebanon.*
> *They are planted in the House of the Lord;*
> *They flourish in the courts of our God."*
> *Ps 92:12-13*

Here we find the key to flourishing and growing in this life; be "***planted in God's house***"!

Making God's house our spiritual home, where we are planted and committed, is the key to growth, health and purpose in this life!

> *"But, speaking the truth in love, may*
> *grow up in all things into Him,*
> *who is the head-Christ-*
> *From whom the whole body,*
> *joined and knit together*
> *by what every joint supplies,*
> *according to the effective working by*
> *which every part does it's share,*
> *causes growth of the body for the*
> *edifying of itself in love."*
> *Ephesians 4:15-16*

Finding 'my place' in God's house is the single most important thing for every believer

Nourishment from Christ through His Body

It is from Christ, the Head of the church, that we find our

place, connect with our people and receive nourishment from each other. God uses people as His channels of nourishment!

Every 'placed member' passes on that nourishment through the relational connections with those who are set around them in the body, or church. This is exactly what the apostle Paul was referring to in Ephesians, when he observed "*every part does it's share*".

Therefore, finding our place in the body of Christ, the church, is not an optional extra! It is vital for the spiritual health and well-being of myself and the other believers that the Lord Jesus Christ connects me to.

> *"And not holding fast the Head,*
> *from whom all the body, nourished and*
> *knit together by joints and ligaments,*
> *grows with the increase that is from God."*
> *Colossians 2:19*

Finding my place in my local church family, the body of Christ, is the direct result of "*holding fast to the Head, Christ*".

Placement provides the believer with following spiritual benefits:-

Placement joins me to God's nourishment method - through *"joints and ligaments"*

Just like our physical bodies, God has designed the body of Christ to have a multitude of *"joints and ligaments"* through which He supplies spiritual nourishment to every believer.

The *"joints"* are two or more members who are joined together in relationship - the point of nourishment.

The *"ligaments"* are the *"bonds of love"* and commitments to each other that hold it all together, that is, the body is *"knit together"* (Colossians 2:19).

Placement protects me with the Body's immunity system

When we are placed in the Body we also find protection by the mutual care and immunity system of the body.

Notice how the writer of Hebrews uses 'body language' to describe the safety and protection from infection, a *"root of bitterness"*, that can *"defile many"*.

This immunity protects the individual members from being "*dislocated*" and provides healing to them.

"Therefore strengthen the
hands which hang down,
and the feeble knees; and make
straight paths for your feet,
so that what is lame may not be
dislocated, but rather be healed.
Pursue peace with all people, and holiness,
without which no one will see the Lord:
Looking carefully lest anyone fall
short of the grace of God;
lest any root of bitterness
springing up cause trouble,
and by this many become defiled."
Hebrews 12:12-15

A healthy Christian is a connected in the church Christian!

Epilogue

THE CHURCH IS STILL GOD'S PLAN

From antiquity the Church has been revealed as the centre piece of God's plan for mankind.

Therefore, there is nothing more important to the Lord Jesus Christ than His Church. The Church is centre in His thoughts, affections, purpose and ultimately revealed in His sacrifice at the cross of Calvary.

> *"Christ loves the Church and*
> *gave Himself for her."*
> *Ephesians 5:25*

The Church is Christ's Work

The work of the Lord Jesus Christ on the earth today is the establishing and building of His Church.

Christ's ultimate intention is to present the church blameless, mature, complete and perfect before Himself and the Father at His second coming.

"That He might sanctify and cleanse it
with the washing of water by the word,
That He might present it to
Himself a glorious church,
not having spot, or wrinkle, or any such thing;
but that it should be holy and without blemish."
Ephesians 5:26-27

The importance of church planting

Therefore, it is through the planting and establishing of millions of local churches that the Gospel of the Lord Jesus Christ will be presented and lived out before a lost world.

Making the church our priority

The moment we commit ourselves to make the church of Christ our love and our priority, we immediately become "*God's fellow workers*" (1Corinthians 3:9). We are aligned with the love, purpose and work of the Lord Jesus Christ in the world.

A faith shared in community

It has never been the will of God that we would live our faith alone and in isolation. Rather, we are to live "*for the faith of the gospel*" together, in connection to and a part of His church family, the House of God.

> "*…that you stand fast in one spirit,*
> *with one mind striving together*
> *for the faith of the gospel.*"
> *Philippians 1:27*

Having read this book it is my sincere prayer that you would be strengthened in your understanding and resolve to find your local church family and make it your priority.

The revelation of the church

It is through a revelation of the house of God, the church, that we know two things:-

First, **WHERE** we belong spiritually; **A MEMBER OF OUR LOCAL CHURCH FAMILY, THE HOUSE OF GOD.**

Second, **HOW** we are to live; **A PRIEST SACRIFICING AND SERVING AS A MEMBER OF THE LOCAL CHURCH, TO *"BUILD UP THE BODY OF CHRIST"*.**

> *"Even so you, since you are*
> *zealous for spiritual gifts,*
> *let it be for the edification (building up)*
> *of the church that you seek to excel."*
> *1Corinthians 14:12*

May your prayer and desire be the same as David the Psalmist:-

> *"One thing have I desired of the*
> *Lord, that will I seek after;*
> *that I may dwell in the house of the*
> *Lord all the days of my life,*
> *to behold the beauty of the Lord,*
> *and to enquire in his temple."*
> *Psalm 27:4*

www.ingramcontent.com/pod-product-compliance
Lightning Source LLC
Chambersburg PA
CBHW071412090426
42737CB00011B/1438

Bibliography

"Burnout in Church Leaders", Peter Kaldor and Rod Bullpit, NCLS Australia

"God's Work", Watchman Nee, Christian Fellowship Publishers, Inc, New York

"Christ the Sum of All Things", Watchman Nee, Christian Fellowship Publishers, Inc, New York

"Tell Your Story", Gordon Moore,

"Strongs Exhaustive Concordance"

"Ellicot's Commentary for English Readers

"Unto Him be glory in the church by Christ Jesus throughout all ages, world without end. Amen."

Ephesians 3:10

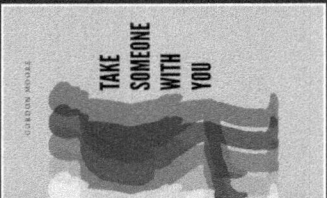

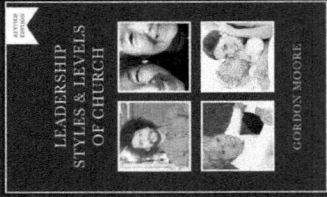